May this story touch you or someone you love —

Allison Richards

Oasis Center Library
317 East Call Street
Tallahassee, Florida 32301

Oasis Center Library
317 East Call Street
Tallahassee, Florida 32301

In His Eyes

Allison Richards
Foreword by Sarah Siciliano-Hartt, Ph.D.

Aurora Publishing
Florida
Delaware

AURORA
PUBLISHING

Copyright © 2007 by Allison Richards
Foreword copyright © 2006 by
Sarah Siciliano-Hartt, Ph.D.
Published by Aurora Publishing

All rights reserved. No part of this book may be reproduced, stored in a retrieval system, or transmitted in any form or by any means, electronic, mechanical, photocopying, recording or otherwise, without the prior permission of the copyright owner.

This book is sold subject to the condition that it shall not, by way of trade or otherwise, be lent, resold, hired out or otherwise circulated without the publisher's prior consent in any form of binding or cover other than that in which it is published and without a similar condition including this condition being imposed on the subsequent purchaser.

Grateful acknowledgement is made to the following for permission to reprint previously published material: Bantam Books, for the excerpts on pages 6, 23, 31, 55, 88, 127, 128, 234, and 274 from S. Forward's and J. Torres' "Men who hate women and the women who love them: When loving hurts and you don't know why" (Copyright © 1986 S. Forward and J. Torres. All Rights Reserved. Used by Permission); Pocket Books/Simon and Scuster, for excerpts on pages 23, 66, 73, 104, 215, and 242 from R. Norwood's "Women who love too much: When you keep wishing and hoping he'll change" (Copyright © 1985 R. Norwood. All Rights Reserved. Used by Permission) and Bob Adams, Inc., for excerpts on pages 29, 93, 101, 131, and 157 from P. Evans' "Verbal abuse survivors speak out" (Copyright © 1993 P. Evans. All Rights Reserved. Used by Permission).

The following is a true story. Although the names have been changed to protect the true identity of the individuals, all other information is factual.

Disclaimer: The author is not a health care professional. She is an emotional abuse survivor. The information and resources in this book are meant to support not replace the advice of a licensed health care or mental health care professional.

Library of Congress Cataloging-in-Publication Data

Richards, Allison.
 In his eyes / Allison Richards ; foreword by Sarah Siciliano-Hartt.
   p. cm.
 ISBN 1-887459-15-4
 1. Family violence. I. Title.

HV6626.R525 2007
362.82'92092--dc22
[B]
            2007002590

Cover designed by Kristen Donlan, JHL Technologies
Printed in Hong Kong

Dedication

This book is lovingly dedicated to my sister Julia, whose compassionate nature knew no bounds.

In His Eyes
A Story of Emotional Abuse and Recovery

TABLE OF CONTENTS

Foreword
    By Sarah Siciliano-Hartt, Ph.D.   13

Part One
    The Early Days   23
        • *Blinders*   28
        • *Why I Left*   31
        • *Why I Returned*   33

Part Two
    Marriage   35
        • *Rejection and Criticism*   40
        • *Control*   43
        • *To Have and To Hold*   45
        • *Strange Behaviors*   50

Part Three
    Pain as a Way of Life   53
        • *A Typical Week*   55
        • *Special Occasions*   60
        • *In Sickness and In Health*   64
        • *Crossing the Line*   70
        • *The Good Times*   75

Part Four
    Waking Up   77
        • *Opening My Eyes*   81
        • *Dark Days*   84
        • *Final Interactions*   90
        • *Learning to Live*   92
        • *Wondering Why*   94

Part Five
    Looking Back   99
        • *My Mother*   101
        • *My Father*   106
        • *Life at Home*   111

Table of Contents cont...

Part Six
    A New Day   121
        • *Learning to Love*   *127*

Postscript
    In My Eyes   133

    Appendix A: Abuse Checklist
    Appendix B: Finding Help
    Appendix C: What to Bring If You Leave
    Appendix D: Recommended Reading

FOREWORD

By Sarah Siciliano-Hartt, Ph.D.

Dr. Sarah Siciliano-Hartt is a licensed psychologist with extensive experience in domestic abuse. She has been in private practice in Florida for over 20 years, and has counseled hundreds of victims of emotional abuse on their journey to recovery.

It has long been acknowledged that victims of abuse, whether physical, sexual or emotional, all suffer a number of adverse consequences. From a physical standpoint, abuse victims can experience direct damage to the body, such as bruising or broken bones, in addition to stress-induced conditions such as headaches or digestive problems. From a sexual standpoint, victims can experience an interruption of normal sexual development, resulting in conditions such as a complete withdrawal from any type of sexual activity or a heightened interest in and pursuit of sexual activity. From an emotional standpoint, abuse victims – whether the abuse is physical, sexual or emotional – are likely to find themselves grappling with recurrent bouts of depression and anxiety throughout the span of their lives. If abuse of whatever form can be viewed as a profound wound to the spirit, then it must follow that abuse victims will suffer in profound ways.

Victims of emotional abuse face an additional set of problems. When a woman is physically abused, she can clearly see direct signs of the abuse (scars, bruises, burns, broken bones, patches of bald spots), which serve as glaring proof that abuse has, in fact, occurred. Sexual abuse victims often have vivid memories of the sexual acts that were committed against them. In many cases, a physical examination provides direct proof of rape or damage to the sexual organs themselves.

Victims of emotional abuse, on the other hand, most often face a more confusing and complex set of circumstances. Let us focus specifically on intimate relationships in adolescence and adulthood. At the outset of the relationship, the abuser typically comes across as a caring, nurturing individual who seeks out and pursues his mate and proceeds to make her the center of his universe. The mate in this case often feels that she has finally found the love of her life. Gradually, cracks begin to develop in this picture. The mate may find that a seemingly minor incident, such as talking to a friend on the phone and being a few minutes late for a date, can precipitate a reaction of rage and vindictiveness. The mate may find that the abuser becomes increasingly jealous of any contact she has with friends or family.

The initial pattern of interacting with a group of friends, joining others for dinner, or traveling with another couple, can gradually be transformed into a rigid routine of one-on-one interactions, with the abuser jealously guarding against the possibility of others intruding upon the scene. Finally, the mate can find that what started out as a steady stream of adoring praise and positive affirmation gives way to occasional verbal swipes that sting in their intensity, and ultimately an endless stream of cutting criticism.

The dilemma that confronts the victim of emotional abuse is a difficult one. Her first impression of the abuser is that he has pursued her and won her. He is the love of her life, the one who will set her life on its intended path of happiness and fulfillment. When events occur that challenge this view, it is a normal reaction for the mate to doubt herself. She must not be viewing this situation from the right perspective, or perhaps she is overreacting. If she does acknowledge that something wrong has occurred, she is likely to look for reasons or circumstances that explain the abuser's behavior and allow him to be placed back on top of his pedestal.

With no direct, physical signs of abuse to ground her in reality, the mate finds herself in an emotional quagmire. To acknowledge that the abuser is mean, jealous, irrational, unreasonable or abusive is to challenge the picture of life that the mate so desperately wants to believe exists. It is far easier for the mate to find fault with herself and to take full responsibility for the difficulties that keep recurring in the relationship. The next step in this self-defeating process is for the mate to exhort herself to try harder. If she were a better person, a more understanding person, a person more capable of anticipating and meeting her lover's needs, none of this would be happening. And thus the downward spiral begins.

As a psychologist in private practice for over 20 years, I have worked with hundreds of victims of emotional abuse. It is from this position that I have read and evaluated Allison Richards' account of her own experience with abuse and recovery. In language that is direct, straightforward and precise, Allison presents a story that resonates with the ring of truth. From the inception of the relationship with Sam in the college years, through the time of her engagement and marriage, up to the point of her decision to leave him, Allison provides detailed descriptions of incidents that clearly portray the relentless pursuit of Sam, the abuser, towards a position of absolute power and control.

Allison's description of the courting period shows how adeptly Sam was able to play the role of the ardent suitor who longed to care for and nurture his newfound love. It is often the initial "golden" impression of the abuser that helps to keep the mate in the relationship long after the abuse has progressed to an intolerable level. Allison's portrayal of the extended period of confusion demonstrates how Sam's fluctuating emotional battering led slowly but steadily to an erosion of her self-worth and self-confidence. Over the course of the marriage, as Sam escalated the level of his abusive behavior, Allison's spirit diminished and she lost her will to live.

It is at this point that Allison made a critical decision. Believing that she needed help to "fix" the relationship so that Sam would switch from hating her to loving her again, she began counseling. Within the individual therapy sessions, Allison began to hear for the first time a trained, objective observer putting forth the idea that the situation at home was not normal. Sam had crossed over the boundary of acceptable behavior and had been brutally abusive for years. As Allison began the process of becoming an observer in her own home, she started to put the pieces together. The picture that emerged was one of lies, selfishness, mental torture and cruelty, all held together by Sam's quest for absolute power and control.

In my view, entering into counseling was the crucial step that led to Allison's recovery. She realized that something was not right and that her life with Sam was draining her will to live. However, the idea that Sam was abusive, the idea that his behavior was unacceptable, the idea that she had options – these "liberating" concepts had not dawned on her. She had become so accustomed to looking at the relationship from Sam's perspective and to seeing things "in his eyes" that she had lost her sense of self. This loss prohibited her from making her own observations, coming to her own conclusions, and voicing her own opinions.

The full recovery process for Allison involved years of therapy and self-analysis. In order to break the cycle of seeking out men who would be abusive, it was necessary for Allison to look back upon her own childhood and examine her relationships with her parents and siblings. It was also essential for Allison to reach out to other victims of emotional abuse, to hear their stories and to share her own.

Today Allison is a happy, emotionally healthy woman, wife and mother. An important part of the recovery process has been the writing of this book. For that, those of us who work with victims of emotional abuse and those who have actually suffered from emotional abuse will be eternally grateful.

Acknowledgments

With deep gratitude, I wish to thank the following:

Jeanette, for taking on this project and working with me every step of the way to make the publishing of this book possible.

"Dr. Sarah," for her enthusiasm and expertise in writing the foreword and her dedication to helping abused women.

Wendy, Christine, and Malinka for their valuable perspectives on the book in its earlier stages.

My children, Brian and Claire, for teaching me about the purest kind of love that life offers.

My husband, Michael, for being everything he seemed to be but I was afraid to believe at first; for giving me time to learn how to trust again; and for always being both at my side and on my side in life.

PART ONE
THE EARLY DAYS

First Impressions
It seemed to be the perfect fairytale romance.

I met Sam at a promising yet naive time in my life. I was twenty years old, a junior at a small liberal arts college in the foothills of South Carolina. I had chosen English as my major since I had always loved to write and spent countless hours reading just for pleasure. Although I was considering becoming an English teacher, I hadn't decided on a definite career path and was just enjoying my first taste of freedom away from home.

I met Sam exactly one week after I had been chosen as a cheerleader for the soccer team. I was eager to make friends with those I considered to be the popular people. I was apprehensive that I wouldn't be accepted as part of their group, so I gladly accepted the invitation when two of the other cheerleaders invited me to accompany them one sunny Friday afternoon in April of 1984.

When we arrived at one of the local pubs, Amanda and Karen seemed to know everyone, but I was feeling a little ill at ease. I had always been shy about meeting new people. In walked Sam with some of the other athletes. His dark hair and eyes instantly reminded me of my father. He seemed so relaxed and confident, laughing and joking around with everyone. Someone suggested we play doubles at pool, and he asked me to be his partner. I was flattered. Soon he was hugging me whenever I made a good shot and making me feel like one of the crowd. It felt a little surreal. Just hours earlier, I had been sort of an outsider in this group. Thanks to Sam, I now felt like I was part of their little club. He made me feel so welcome, and I was starting to sense a mutual attraction forming. The afternoon soon turned to evening, and I was having the time of my life.

We had all worked up ravenous appetites after socializing all afternoon, so someone suggested we head to the college cafeteria for dinner. I ended up sitting next to Sam, and we talked effortlessly the entire time. The others seemed to fade into the background as we enjoyed getting to know one another. I found out that he, too, was Catholic and that he was considering a career in teaching. When he told me he was majoring in biology, I was impressed because science classes had always been a challenge for me. I could tell that he was well educated by his impeccable grammar, and this made him even more attractive to me.

That night Sam drove me back to the dormitory and kissed me goodnight, slowly and with such tenderness. I felt weak in my knees. Whatever was happening felt wonderful and almost too good to be true. I was afraid that this would be the end of it, one fun-filled evening. But the next day, he was waiting for me at the cafeteria. He smiled at me and took my hand. From that day on we were a couple.

The relationship progressed quickly, but at the time it felt exciting and as though it were just meant to be. Sam seemed to be crazy about me. After only three weeks, he told me that he wanted to marry me someday! I questioned him about how we barely knew each other, but he insisted that it was God's will to bring us together and that he'd been waiting all of his life for a girl like me. He called his mother on the telephone right in front of me and said, "Mom, I want you to talk to the girl I'm going to marry."

The first several months flew by like a whirlwind. Sam wanted to spend every possible moment with me. My friends at the dormitory were so impressed with his romantic nature. He was constantly bringing me flowers, writing poetry about me, and taking me out for candlelight dinners. But it was deeper than just the romance. We spent countless hours just talking. We discussed our families, our beliefs and values, what we wanted to do with our lives. We both had an interest in traveling to other countries and learning as much as we could about the world. But he also expressed a strong desire to have children and wanted to make his family the top priority in his life. It seemed he was instinctively saying just what I wanted to hear. I was impressed with his strong faith, as spirituality was a very important part of my life.

Sam invited me to meet his family, and I was just as eager to introduce him to mine. His parents were very warm and welcoming, and his sister seemed quiet but friendly enough. He pulled me aside after only an hour and told me that they loved me and couldn't wait to include me as part of their family. When I introduced him to my family, they were quite impressed with his impeccable manners and gentlemanly nature. They sensed that I was happy, so they had no qualms about welcoming him in our home.

The chemistry between us was strong and constant. I was attracted to his soft brown eyes and athletic build. I remember noticing how his dark complexion looked so beautiful against my fair, freckled skin. When he kissed me I felt he was giving me a part of his soul. Our intimacy developed naturally. There was no awkwardness that sometimes accompanies a new partnership; it felt as though we'd been together for years even though it had only been a few months.

One night we were on our way to a formal dance with another couple. Sam said he had forgotten something in his dormitory and told them we'd meet them at the dance hall. When we got to his room he confessed that he was just trying to steal some time alone with me, and that he wanted to make love. It would have been our first time. I wanted to more than anything, but I had long ago decided I would wait until I was married, or at least engaged. I was afraid that he wouldn't understand. To my surprise and delight, Sam shared that he was a virgin too and that he respected me even more for wanting to wait. At that point I knew that Sam was far more mature than the others I had dated, and I felt that his love for me was undoubtedly sincere given his understanding and willingness to wait. It seemed to be the perfect fairytale romance.

Blinders
Blinders serve the function of eliminating from your vision any information that might cloud or spoil your romantic picture.
(From "Men Who Hate Women and the Women Who Love Them")

As the months passed, Sam's devotion remained as constant as ever, but a deep jealousy began to surface when I least expected it. What had once felt like devotion started to feel more like a demand for my undivided and constant attention. One weekend he went out of town and arrived back at school much earlier than either of us had anticipated. I had gone to dinner with some friends, planning to return by the time I originally expected him to arrive. I never heard from him that night. The next morning when I saw him on my way to class, he would hardly speak to me. He became very sarcastic and accused me of having been out with someone else since I wasn't waiting in my dormitory when he arrived. I was surprised that he would come to this conclusion, and assured him that this was not the case. I thought he knew how much I loved him.

Sam became very distant for a few days, and then suddenly everything was back to normal again. I shrugged it off, assured that it would be the exception rather than the rule in our relationship. But just when I would least expect it, I'd get the cold shoulder from him again, sometimes for days at a time. One night he left me at a bar because he said I was dancing too provocatively. Another time he kept track of the time I spent lifting weights with a male friend who was coaching me, and accused me of lying about what I'd "really been doing for the last two hours."

Although I knew that Sam's jealousy was unfounded, I began to wonder if perhaps I was being too careless with his feelings. I couldn't believe that someone so loving and caring could also be so cold and unreasonable. I believed that I could help him to trust me and that these problems wouldn't exist given enough time. I started to limit my time with male friends and constantly reassured Sam of my devotion to him, but my efforts didn't seem to make a difference. Even something as innocent as the mention of an ex-boyfriend in casual conversation would result in moodiness and the silent treatment. I felt hurt and confused. I felt unable to convince him that he had nothing to worry about.

Soon I started to notice other things about Sam that disturbed me. He tended to lie about things, not to me as far as I knew, but to his coach, his friends, his professors. When I told him that it bothered me, he laughed and said that everyone does it. Then one afternoon he told me he needed a favor from me. He had received several parking tickets over the year, and his grades would not be released until the bill was paid. He didn't have the money and asked me if I'd help him to "take care of the situation." I thought he wanted me to loan him the money, so I was shocked when he revealed his plan to break into the office at night and remove the ticket files. I couldn't believe he would be so dishonest. He didn't seem like the same person who had attended church with me just the night before. I refused to help and he didn't become angry as I had feared. In fact, he seemed relieved and I began to wonder if he was just testing me in some strange way since I had recently expressed concern over his dishonesty.

I tried to dismiss the discomfort I had started to feel about how well I actually knew Sam and exactly what kind of person he really was. One night he took me to dinner at a beautiful restaurant and we were having a wonderful time. Any problems between us seemed distant and cloudy, as though they weren't really a part of our lives. We shared some wine and started to talk about our high school years. I told him that I wasn't very confident in high school and had felt very intimidated by the "in" crowd. He shared that he had felt the same way. We seemed so in sync and intimate again. Then he laughed and said that there were other things about him that I might not find so endearing. He shared that he had been arrested in high school for stealing from a gas station, and that in every job he had held since, he had considered it a challenge to see if he could get away with stealing something. My heart sank and the room seemed to spin. I didn't know what to say or how to react. I wanted him to say it was all a joke. I told him that I felt sick and needed to leave.

I didn't want to end my relationship with Sam; I was in love. I told myself that I was overreacting to what he had shared. He was still telling me several times a day how much he loved me, still sending flowers, still writing letters filled with beautiful expressions of his love for me. What I did try to do was communicate with him about behaviors that upset or sometimes even alarmed me. I soon learned that Sam was not willing to talk to me if it involved anything remotely critical of him or his behavior. He labeled my attempts to communicate as trying to control him and would withdraw from me for days at a time. I started to feel extremely off-balance, apologizing for no reason just to win his love back and wondering what I had done to lose it in the first place.

I kept asking myself, which was the real Sam? Was he the loving, tender, affectionate one or the jealous, angry, silent one? I wanted to believe the first. It had to be the first so that I could keep loving him and accepting his love for me. And so the blinders went on for the next two years.

Why I Left
*What had happened to the love we shared
only a few short years ago?*

Nearly two years passed. I graduated from college and returned to my hometown to look for a job. I was hired as an editor at a market research firm and was excited to be starting a career. But my enthusiasm paled in comparison to the sadness I had started to feel about my relationship with Sam. He had one year left before completing college, and had transferred to a school in Florida to be closer to his family. We were now living 600 miles apart and only saw each other about once a month on weekends. Even though we kept in close touch through letters and phone calls, it seemed as though Sam assumed he "had" me by now since we had long since agreed we'd marry someday. The expressions of love that had once flowed between us so naturally were all coming from me now, with little to no return.

From time to time, he would be as wonderful and loving as he'd been in the beginning, but more often than not he seemed to have become nonchalant if not downright careless about our relationship. If I became upset about something, he'd refuse to discuss it. My need to talk openly about our relationship simply went unmet, as I had learned that even the suggestion of such a conversation would result in the withdrawal of his love and affection. I became depressed and anxious, and began to feel as though I were walking on eggshells most of the time. I wanted to recapture the love we'd had before but felt helpless to do so. I just couldn't put my finger on why things had changed.

There seemed to be an underlying anger in Sam that was prepared to erupt at a moment's notice. Even when nothing was wrong, I often felt that he was angry with me or maybe that he was just angry in general. I couldn't tell the difference. He became extremely sarcastic, making snide remarks for no apparent reason yet refusing to admit he was upset about anything. I was bewildered and confused by Sam's mixed messages. He'd tell me he wasn't angry then refuse to talk to me. He once showed up at my dormitory and handed me a stack of pictures of us together, saying that he no longer had any need for them. I thought he was breaking up with me, but he insisted that I was the only one for him. It made no sense. Another time he confessed that he had kissed someone else, then began laughing and said the story was just a joke.

The final straw was the night he told me over the phone that he still wanted to marry me someday, but that he'd like to be free to date around until then. It shocked me into realizing what a confused person he was and how little he valued our relationship. I felt my heart sink and my eyes fill with huge tears. What had happened to the love we shared only a few short years ago? But my pride stepped in and I refused to go along with his suggested arrangement. I think he was as shocked as I was when I told him I wanted to end our relationship. I hung up the phone and collapsed on the floor sobbing.

The next day was a day of grief for me. I mourned for the relationship that had once looked so promising, for the plans we had made, for the love I'd thought I found. But then a strange thing happened. I started to feel a sense of relief now that I was no longer in emotional pain or walking on eggshells. I felt lighter and less stressed than I had in the three years that Sam and I were together.

A few months passed, and the feeling of relief continued. I was indeed happier without Sam. But just as I was starting to realize what a strain the relationship had been on me, Sam was becoming more and more determined to win me back. He mailed letters to me almost daily, begging me to reconsider and apologizing for having hurt me. But I wasn't ready to give him another chance. I had finally begun to feel like myself again.

Why I Returned
*He claimed he had grown up, I claimed he had
come to his senses, and we both agreed
it was nothing short of a miracle.*

Six months passed, and slowly but surely Sam began to convince me that he had truly changed. He no longer seemed angry or sarcastic, and he actually wanted to communicate with me and talk about our feelings! In fact, he insisted that we discuss every single thing he'd done in the past that had caused me pain. As icing on the cake, he attributed all of these changes to his renewed relationship with God. He wanted to pray together as a couple and talk to a priest if we had any problems we couldn't handle alone. He told me he had gone to confession to be cleansed of all the hurtful things he had done and said to me in the past.

I felt as though the love we had shared before really had been authentic, that we had somehow just misunderstood each other but were being given a second chance! I had that feeling in my stomach like I had felt the first day we met; the attraction and excitement had returned. Sam even told me we could just stay friends for awhile if I wasn't comfortable getting back together at this point, but I was eager to begin our new relationship. I felt that my original impressions about Sam had been accurate after all.

The year that followed was filled with joy, as Sam and I were more in love than ever. He even moved to my hometown so that we wouldn't have to be apart so much. I'd find little love notes he'd left in my purse, flowers would arrive at the office, and the love was flowing again. The most important difference in our relationship was that he talked things through with me whenever we had a misunderstanding, and never seemed cold or distant as he had in the past. Although a few flashbacks of anger and jealousy occurred, I wrote them off as the normal difficulties people occasionally experience in relationships. Sam even shared with me a journal he'd kept while we were apart and shortly after we had reunited. I was more certain than ever that we were meant to be together when I read what he'd written about our relationship:

> *I think we really appreciate each other more now, and I can't wait to marry her and spend the rest of my life with her. There is absolutely no way I will ever again do anything to lose her. We communicate so much better now. I just can't see us having the same problems as we have had in the past. I know we have so much to look forward to - a life full of sharing, learning about each other, growing together as one. This time, I know what I have to do to make things turn out right. I don't think it's often that people get a second chance at love like I have. I'm not about to find out if there are third chances. I'm ready to do the right thing this time to ensure our happiness forever...*

I believed the mysterious and disturbing anger I had once sensed in Sam was gone. He claimed he had grown up, I claimed he had come to his senses, and we both agreed it was nothing short of a miracle.

PART TWO
MARRIAGE

We may cry and scream and weep and wail. But we are not able to use our emotions to guide us in making the necessary and important choices in our life.
(From "Women Who Love Too Much"*)*

Sam and I had been back together for over a year. After being unable to secure a teaching job in South Carolina, he had finally landed a job as a middle school teacher at an excellent school in Florida. Although I was heartbroken that he'd be leaving, I knew that this was a wise choice for him in regard to his career. He asked me to move with him, but it didn't seem right for me to leave the security of my own job and family when we had not worked out any details on when we'd get married or what kind of career I would pursue in Florida. Although it seemed understood that we'd marry someday, we had never actually discussed when, where, or any other details. I had always fantasized that he'd surprise me with a diamond ring, and this certainly seemed like the perfect time.

My birthday was only a few months away when Sam's mother called to confide in me that he had asked her advice about purchasing a diamond for me. She knew he wanted it to be a surprise, but she wanted to know if I had any preferences on style. I was so thrilled to hear that he was planning to propose that the style of diamond was the furthest issue from my mind. My birthday arrived and I could hardly contain my enthusiasm but was determined to act surprised. Sam brought over a beautiful stuffed lion, and I instantly noticed the sparkling diamond earrings he had placed on the lion's ears. I loved the earrings, but still believed he had a ring for me and was just waiting for the perfect moment to propose. The next morning, it was difficult for me to conceal my disappointment, so I ended up confessing the entire story to Sam. He was furious with both his mother and me. He jumped up and starting yelling, telling me that I had no right to expect him to spend that much money on me and that I was an ingrate for not being appreciative of the earrings. He said that his mother must have misunderstood him and that he never intended to give me a diamond ring, not now and not ever. I was stunned. I felt such a mixture of emotions: sadness and disappointment that my dreams of being proposed to were so far from reality, guilt that I had betrayed his mother's confidence and caused him to become so angry, and confusion over why this was such a big deal to him. Finally, I felt a familiar twinge that sickened my stomach: he was acting like the old Sam, the angry Sam, the Sam I thought we had left behind us.

A few days passed and finally Sam asked me to talk. He told me how hurt he was that I wasn't excited about the earrings. He said that he would buy a ring for me if it was that important to me. I felt so guilty that I had upset and hurt him. I was so relieved that he had approached me and talked through his feelings. I convinced myself that the old Sam would not have done this and therefore he really had changed for the better. I convinced myself that I had nothing to worry about.

Six months later, Sam surprised me with a beautiful diamond ring on Easter Sunday. I was ecstatic, so much so that I told him I wanted to make love for the first time. He had waited so patiently and now I knew that he was going to be my husband. It was time. I cooked spaghetti and we had wine. We toasted to our new life together as husband and wife. I thought I would be nervous, but all I felt was an abundance of love for Sam and eager anticipation for us to become even closer than we had been before. It was beautiful and loving. He told me afterwards that he wanted to get married as soon as possible so that we could be together every night. We both cried and held each other, and I realized that I had never been so happy in my life.

As the wedding plans began in earnest, I noticed that Sam was happy to let me make all of the decisions about location, who to invite, what to serve. He seemed to have confidence in me, which made me feel even more secure about our future. The planning went smoothly, and we were able to schedule our wedding for only four months after we had become engaged. Everything was falling into place beautifully.

Other than Sam catching a glimpse of me in my wedding gown a few hours before the ceremony, at which point we both just smiled and he mouthed "I love you" to me, our wedding day couldn't have gone any more smoothly. When I walked down the aisle to greet him, he whispered to me that I looked like an angel. He kept licking his lips with nervousness but couldn't stop smiling throughout the ceremony. So many of our guests commented on how happy we both looked and told us that the ceremony brought tears to their eyes.

The hotel I had chosen for our wedding night had a huge balcony overlooking a river. We stood outside and looked at the stars. I told him how happy I was. He looked a little annoyed and said that he was tired. I was tired too, but it was our wedding night and I wanted it to be special. I put on a beautiful white gown I had received at my wedding shower, and we made love until we both fell asleep in happy exhaustion.

Rejection and Criticism
He used for weapons his words and his moods.
(*From* "Men Who Hate Women and the Women Who Love Them")

One week after our wedding, Sam became withdrawn and sullen, and refused to speak with me for two days. All he would tell me was that he was unhappy. He wouldn't say why, and any attempt to talk or be affectionate with him were met with a firm and unwavering rejection. He would physically push me away if I tried to hug him and would walk into another room if I suggested that we discuss what was bothering him.

A few days later Sam snapped out of this mood and appeared happy again. However, at any moment the silence would return for no apparent reason. I began to look for ways to ensure he'd be happy and I questioned everything I did or said to figure out what might upset him. I apologized for things I had no business being sorry for and became more confused than ever. We were both unhappy, and I couldn't figure out what was going on. I lived like a detective, believing that if I could only discover what made him happy and avoid doing whatever made him unhappy, I'd have the key to making this marriage work.

The communication skills Sam had been so eager to learn while we were engaged simply seemed to disappear once we were married. He announced at one point that I should not waste my time apologizing for anything because apologies meant nothing to him. The attempts he did make at communication were degrading and sarcastic. If he had decided to reconcile with me after a period of unexplained silence, he'd come to me and announce that he was ready for me to beg for his forgiveness.

Sam's rejection of me, whether it was my apologies, my affection or my attempts to communicate, began to wear me down. I believed he had stopped loving me and I couldn't figure out why. I felt an incredible sadness. And yet, I had made a commitment to a lifetime with him that I intended to keep. And so I forged on and continued to work at our relationship. But dealing with the rejection was only a small piece of the challenge that lay before me. Once we were married, I became the object of Sam's relentless and often cruel criticism. He criticized everything from my appearance to my education to my family. Although I was never even slightly overweight, he made constant remarks about my size. When I tried to tell him how much this offended me, he said that I couldn't take a joke and that it was vain of me to always want to be complimented.

One evening we were going to a surprise party for one of his co-workers, and I was excited to be all dressed up. As we were leaving the house, a neighbor commented that I looked pretty. When we got into the car, Sam immediately commented that he was dreading having his friends see him with such a haggish wife. On another occasion, we were attending a friend's wedding. After complimenting his sister and his mother on how great they looked, he added that "even my wife looks almost presentable today."

It seemed that anything I took pride in became a target for Sam's derogatory comments. He insisted that my college degree didn't count and that my family was ignorant and behind the times. His constant belittling knew no bounds and I began to feel self-conscious about every move I made. He labeled me clumsy, ignorant and wimpy. He mocked the way I drove, the way I walked, the way I ate, even the way I smiled.

I believe that Sam felt he had to whittle down my self-confidence in order to feel better about himself. Our wedding seemed to have marked the beginning of losing my sense of self and painfully adjusting my opinions and perceptions to those of Sam's in order to keep the peace. His criticisms of me started to become my reality until I almost despised myself as much as he seemed to despise me. I had begun the journey to living "in his eyes."

Control

His motive is to control you, not to be with you in a mutual way, and his strategy is to diminish you so you will doubt yourself and be more controllable.
(*From* "Verbal Abuse Survivors Speak Out")

It seemed that once Sam was convinced I no longer had the will, the energy, or the confidence to challenge him, he began taking control of nearly every aspect of our life together. Although we both earned nearly the same salary, he took complete control of the money and doled it out to me only as he saw fit, while he spent freely on himself. He established what he called the house rules, which consisted of nearly impossible standards of neatness. He became furious if what he had designated as my bathroom became even slightly in need of cleaning. He claimed the master bathroom as his own and forbade me to use it, yet insisted that I clean it. He would inspect every inch of the shower and demand that the floor mats be lined up on a particular row of tiles. Anything less was considered a breech of cooperation on my part.

Sam's control filtered down to even the smallest details of housekeeping. Pillows must be fluffed and placed in a certain position at all times, dining room chairs must be properly pushed in immediately after eating. He even complained that my clothing was not well organized in the closet. Sam decided what items went on the grocery list, when the shopping and laundry should be done, and when we would accept invitations to go out with friends. Any decisions I made without him were met with the accusation that I was being inconsiderate of his feelings, yet he never consulted with me on my preferences or opinions. He considered all of our belongings his, even though most of our possessions had been purchased mutually.

Sam even tried to control what our life would be like once we had children. He made it clear that he would not take care of me if I were sick during pregnancy, that I was responsible for making sure the children did not disrupt his sleeping schedule, and that I was expected to be back at work less than six weeks after I had the baby. He didn't want any toys scattered around the house, and announced that he'd be miserable for the first few years because of the inconveniences.

At this point, the future looked pretty bleak, but I still believed I could make a happy home for us and for our future children. I thought that if I just honored his requests to be considerate of his feelings, he'd begin to be considerate of mine.

To Have and To Hold
It was closer to a rape than a loving experience…

Since Sam was my first lover, I had no real frame of reference for what making love should be like. But I did know that what we were doing did not feel pleasurable or loving anymore. It wasn't romantic or emotionally fulfilling the way it had been during our engagement. In fact, I started to feel violated and empty, and eventually I felt nothing at all.

When we were engaged, Sam had told me that his main concern about sex was that he wanted to please and satisfy me. He said if he could do this, he'd be happy. And he was a considerate lover at first, but that changed abruptly. Only a short time after our wedding, he didn't come near me for almost six weeks: no sex, no kissing, nothing. I was starving for affection.

I attributed his behavior to the difficulties we were having adjusting to being married. It soon became apparent that no matter whether we were getting along well or not, Sam could go for weeks or sometimes well over a month with no apparent desire to make love with me. If I approached him, he'd turn me down and accuse me of being a nymphomaniac. But when he decided he was interested, he would move in on me like an animal. Somewhere along the way he had stopped kissing me. Then the foreplay disappeared almost completely. When he wanted me, he'd just grab me, usually from behind, no matter where I was in the house or what I was doing. Many times he would already be naked from the waist down and I was supposed to be ready right then and there. If he wanted to change positions, he'd just throw me around like a rag doll, never asking what I wanted. He actually told me that he preferred positions where he would not have to look at my face.

Sam usually didn't stop long enough for me to fully disrobe. In fact, I don't think he really even knew what my breasts looked like. It never lasted any length of time either. The whole episode, start to finish, was usually four minutes or less. It was closer to a rape than a loving experience, but those four minutes were the closest thing to intimacy that I was getting. Some tenderness returned from time to time, but was never sustained.

Sometimes Sam would decide he wanted to have sex in public places. It was not the spirit of spontaneity that seemed to drive him, but rather the element of control. He felt he was entitled to have me sexually at any time or place without question. When I felt uncomfortable and rejected his advances, he'd tell me I was boring and had no sense of adventure. Once we were playing miniature golf in the middle of the afternoon, and he decided we should have sex on the course. There were families with children all around us. He pointed to a small grassy area that was partially hidden from the course and told me to lie down. I remember looking up at the sunny sky and feeling branches poking at my spine. He laid on top of me and it started. I could hear the cheerful voices of the other patrons approaching. I told him that we could get arrested for indecent exposure and asked him to stop. He jumped up and walked away, leaving me stunned and confused. It took me ten minutes to find him. He had gone ahead on the course and started playing golf again without me. He refused to acknowledge me, so I headed to the finishing area and waited for him, wondering once again why he was so angry.

Ironically, my attempts to improve our sex life were met with contempt. He seemed equally disgusted and intimidated by any expression of my own needs. Once I suggested that we take pictures of each other in front of the Christmas tree; nothing offensive, just some tasteful shots of me in lingerie or him in boxer shorts. I was hungry for some element of fun, and I wanted to feel sexy and appreciated. He was shocked and disgusted. Another time I dressed in a beautiful red negligee I had received from my bridal shower. I put it on while I was cooking dinner to surprise him when he arrived home from work. When he walked in and saw me, he immediately went into the bedroom and closed the door. He didn't come out until dinner was ready. He sat down and told me that he wouldn't be able to eat unless I agreed to change into something decent.

Sam had a way of making me seem cheap or vulgar when it came to my sexuality. When any of our male friends would pay me a compliment, he'd respond as though I were a possession of his: "Oh, you think she's pretty? Well, you can have her if you want." As time went on, Sam lost almost all interest in intercourse and began demanding that I just give him oral sex. If I complained, he'd order me to "get down there and get to work." I always hoped that if I did this for him, he'd reward me with some type of affection. Occasionally it happened. More often than not, though, he'd try to cover me completely with the bed sheets so that he wouldn't have to look at me. Sometimes I had trouble breathing, but if I'd try to remove the sheet he'd force my head back down to where he wanted it. Soon he started requesting that I do this for him while he was watching television. If I refused he'd tell me that I was insecure and selfish, and ignore me for a few days. I became like a robot, lifelessly performing these tasks to avoid the inevitable silence that would follow if I refused him.

Sam frequented strip clubs with his friends. When I told him how much this bothered me, he accused me of trying to control him. Sam had no qualms about openly staring at other women while he was with me. He even brought home magazines for singles and circled the ads he found appealing. He'd leave them in clear view on the kitchen counter for me to see. I doubt if he ever intended to follow up on the ads, but this undermined my confidence and created a window of doubt as to how far he'd go if he wasn't happy with me.

Many times after we had sex, Sam seemed to become very childlike and frightened. He'd grab the blanket, wrap himself up in it, and curl up in a ball in the corner of the room or even in the closet. I never knew how to react. He wouldn't respond to me if I talked to him. He'd just look at me with big, frightened eyes.

I started thinking about Sam's relationship with his sister, Rachel. It had always seemed strange and unnatural to me, but I had never given it much thought. When he first brought me to his home to meet his family, he had warned me that Rachel would not like me. He said she became very jealous whenever he dated anyone. After being standoffish initially, Rachel soon became friendly with me and we grew to be very close friends. One night while Sam was out of town, Rachel invited me to spend the night at her house. We stayed up late talking about all kinds of things, and she told me she wanted to share something with me that she had never told anyone. She told me that Sam used to climb into bed with her and cuddle when they were children, and that she thinks something sexual may have happened between them.

I immediately flashed back to the night before our wedding. Sam had called me crying, saying that he wasn't sure he could leave his sister. He said she'd been in her room for hours playing the same song over and over. It was a love song. I was so confused; what did his sister have to do with our relationship? He seemed to calm down, and I put it out of my mind. I had a wedding to look forward to.

A few years later when Rachel married, she insisted that her first dance, a love song, be with Sam. Her husband later approached me and asked if I thought their relationship was strange. He told me that he often felt like a third wheel around them and wanted to know if I felt the same. He told me he was worried because after only a few months of marriage, she was unable to look at him when they had sex and could only make love in total darkness. I could offer him no explanation other than my agreement that their relationship seemed unnatural. Rachel had never again acknowledged our late night conversation, and I didn't feel comfortable approaching her or Sam about it. I knew that something was desperately wrong here, but I just couldn't piece it all together.

Strange Behaviors

Their awareness of their mate's hostile behavior was often clouded by the shadows of shock, confusion, and pain.
(*From* "Verbal Abuse Survivors Speak Out")

Perhaps the most unnerving aspect of my marriage to Sam was the unpredictability of his moods and behavior. He said and did things that I found odd, disturbing, even terrifying, with complete composure and no apparent remorse. He lied to me, to his friends, his family, co-workers, even to perfect strangers. Sometimes he'd lie for convenience, sometimes for financial gain, but often it seemed he lied simply as a means of control. To get away with it seemed a small but significant victory to him. I'll never know for sure how much of what he told me was true, but on several occasions I confronted him about lying to me. His response was that he lied either because he just felt like it, or that he had to lie because I would overreact to the truth.

Then I discovered that Sam was constantly stealing. He seemed to believe that he was entitled to anything he could get his hands on. Again, getting away with stealing seemed to represent a strange sort of victory and confirmation of control for him. He stole only things we had no need for: sod from a neighbor's yard, office furniture from his workplace, even golf clubs and sunglasses from his friends. Sometimes he'd even wrap up something he had taken from a friend and present it to him years later as a gift, just to watch the person's reaction. I recalled our conversation at a restaurant one night when we were dating, and how I had justified his confessions about stealing by telling myself that he had simply made mistakes because he was young and immature.

Social events were another arena of unpredictability and frequent embarrassment. Sam could be friendly, well-mannered and outgoing one minute and completely childish the next. When

I invited him to the annual office picnic, he refused to socialize with anyone. When I tried to approach him he literally ran away from me, climbed a nearby tree, and refused to come down. At a holiday party at my boss' house, Sam began to walk away from me every time I tried to approach him. I spent hours trying to corner him just so that we could leave.

Perhaps the most disturbing of all of Sam's strange behaviors was what is often called gaslighting, or setting someone up to believe he or she is becoming insane. Sam would methodically set up situations that he would then use to justify his anger and blame towards me. He'd throw away important documents or pieces of mail and then approach me to ask where I'd put them. When I'd insist that I had left something in a certain location, he'd direct me to the trash can and demand an explanation for my carelessness. Sam once planted his set of keys in my purse right before I left to visit my family. When I called to let him know I'd arrived, he told me that I had ruined his weekend by leaving him without access to a car, and that he didn't want to talk to me again until I returned home. Another time he moved my bike to a remote location in a shopping center just so that he could convince me that I'd been careless enough to allow it to be stolen.

Sam also seemed to take great pleasure in frightening me. One evening when I was home alone and he knew I wasn't expecting him for some time, he began to pound on the front door of our apartment with his fists. Just as I was about to call the police, he began laughing hysterically. When I asked why he would want to frighten me, he answered that it was fun for him to see my reaction.

Underneath each of Sam's strange and disturbing behaviors seemed to be a desire to maintain control over my emotions, my actions, and my world.

PART THREE
PAIN AS A WAY OF LIFE

[W]hat feels good and what feels bad have become confused and entangled and finally one and the same.
(From "Women Who Love Too Much"*)*

By the end of the first year of our marriage, my spirit was nearly broken. I no longer fought for my rights with my former conviction and enthusiasm. Very few of Sam's behaviors shocked me anymore, though they never ceased to disturb me. I still believed things were not right, but a strange acceptance had crept in, allowing me to survive without truly living and to keep the peace rather than make a point.

Between the mind games and the gradual brainwashing, I had learned to doubt nearly all of my original perceptions about what a loving marriage should be like, and I had begun to live "in his eyes," while mine lay softly shut for three more years.

A Typical Week
No matter how much you give, or give up, it is never enough.
(*From* "Men Who Hate Women and the Women Who Love Them")

I'd bolt out of bed at six-thirty every weekday morning and rush to the kitchen to make a lunch for Sam to take to work. I was careful to be very cheerful about this task because if I revealed the slightest sign of irritation, he'd state that I obviously didn't care enough about him, insist on doing it himself, and then quit speaking to me until I'd practically beg him to let me do it again. I was also expected to make his breakfast and to have it waiting for him when I awakened him. If I put out a fork or spoon he didn't like, he'd call to me and I was expected to exchange it immediately for one he found acceptable.

When he was ready to leave for work, Sam would stand at the front door and call for me. I was to come immediately and kiss him goodbye; that is, as long as he was happy with me. If this was a silent time when he was angry with me for some reason, he'd just leave without saying goodbye. Whoever arrived home first cooked dinner, but it was always to be served by me. As soon as we'd sit down to eat, he'd turn on the television. I wasn't supposed to talk to him except during commercials. Sometimes he'd want to talk about his day. If he'd had a particularly good day, he might even listen to something about mine. But many times after I'd relate a story of something that had happened at the office, he'd just give me a blank stare and say, "Do you think I care?"

I got used to it. Sometimes I even laughed, or started my conversation with, "I know you don't really care, but I'm going to tell you this anyway..." But when it involved something really important, it got to me. I remember the day I found out I'd received a major promotion at work. I wanted so much for him to be happy for me. He wasn't. I justified his behavior by telling myself he felt badly because his career wasn't advancing as quickly as he had hoped.

After dinner, Sam would open the mail. It was established in the first month of our marriage that I could only open mail addressed to me. I had made the mistake of opening our first electric bill. When he saw it lying on the counter he became furious. He shoved the envelope in my face and said, "Do you see your name on this?" This was early on, when I was just beginning to see him in a different light, so I became equally furious. I stood up for my rights to open our mutual bills. A silent dinner followed, then a silent evening, a silent morning. My attempts to talk with him about it were rejected, as were my attempts at affection.

After two days of silence, a credit card bill arrived. I was too tired, drained and confused for another fight. I didn't open it. After he saw it unopened on the counter, the silence ended, the affection returned, and he loved me again. Although I never opened another bill, mail time still made my stomach turn at least once a month when the phone bill arrived. He'd read aloud each of the long-distance charges to my family. I was paying for these calls with my own money, but somehow it was still presented as some type of offense.

Sometimes I'd watch television with Sam after I'd finished the dishes, but it had to be what he wanted to watch. If I really insisted on watching one of my favorite shows, he'd make fun of the show and comment on how all the women were bitches. If I wanted to go to bed early, he'd insist that I stay up with him and sleep next to him on the couch while he watched television. Then after I'd fallen asleep he'd sneak off to bed by himself. But first he'd go around the entire house and turn on all of the lights and open all of the blinds so that I'd have plenty of work to do before coming to bed myself. If I refused to stay up with him and went to bed first, he'd come into the bedroom, turn on the lights and blare the stereo, then walk out. He'd continue to do this as many times as necessary until I'd give in. I even tried locking the bedroom door but he'd easily unlock it. It became a strange game we played. It became the norm.

Friday night always came too quickly. We'd go to dinner at a local restaurant and sit as close to the big screen TV as possible. Again, he'd only talk to me during commercials. Then came the weekly trip to the grocery store. He'd insist that all of the items in the cart be lined up perfectly. If I was walking in front of him, he'd often push the cart into me, not playfully, but hard enough to hurt and embarrass me.

I often noticed others feeling embarrassed for me when they observed his strange treatment of me. If he spotted something at the checkout counter that was not on his list, he'd question me loudly about why I thought I needed that item. Putting the groceries away was also a tedious task. All labels had to face forward and all items must be stored according to size. Friday night had also been deemed laundry night. Whenever he was separating the clothes, he'd literally throw my clothes at me, usually aiming for my face. Soon he began doing the same thing with my keys.

Every Saturday morning for years I awakened to the same words: "It's time for you to make my breakfast." After breakfast he'd leave the dishes for me and go off to play basketball or golf with his friends. I was expected to clean the house, top to bottom, before he arrived home. I found that if I didn't stop to take any breaks I could finish in a little over four hours. He'd arrive home in the afternoon, ready to have his lunch fixed and to perform the ritual inspection of the house.

Sam wasn't usually interested in doing anything social on weekend evenings. Sometimes we did go out with friends, but more often we spent Saturday nights at a nearby mall. He'd want to look for purchases for himself, and somehow there was never enough time for me to look around for myself. If I'd suggest that we separate and meet at a designated time, he'd physically restrain me from leaving his side. Once I insisted on trying on a blouse I wanted for work. I guess he thought I took too long in the dressing room. When I stepped out to get his opinion, he started yelling at me in front of everyone, questioning what had taken me so long.

And so the weeks and months along with the seasons came and went. This rollercoaster type of relationship gradually became the expected and the norm. As I recall all of these events, it is difficult to believe I would ever stoop to such depths, to allow myself to be treated this way. No one who knew me would have believed it. But as I came to learn later, this was all part of the sickness of an abusive cycle. When you truly believe that your entire well-being depends on securing the love of another person, and when that person is abusive and convincing enough, almost nothing seems too demeaning at the time.

I became convinced that I was indebted to Sam because of all he was doing for me. I believed this because he told me this hundreds of times, year after year. He reminded me daily of everything he did for me. He told me that he had given me a better life than I could've ever had with my own family. If he became displeased because a meal wasn't on time or a sandwich wasn't up to his standards, I learned to believe that I wasn't trying hard enough to do a good job at showing my appreciation for him.

Probably the greatest motivating factor was the knowledge that deviation from these unwritten rules meant immediate rejection, silence, and the withdrawal of Sam's love. That translated to unbearable pain for me. My perceptions had already been distorted for so long that there was no way for me to see anything objectively. My reasoning was that if I could somehow just do things the way he liked, he'd be happy with me and he'd love me the way he did before we were married. That was my fantasy, but unfortunately that was all it ever amounted to.

Special Occasions
They had lost their previous appeal and become days I simply wanted to make it through.

Our first holiday season as husband and wife was a disaster. We had agreed to spend the holidays with my family that year, but later Sam outright refused to go. I went alone, intending to return on Christmas Eve. An unexpected snowstorm prevented me from returning until the day after Christmas. When I called Sam on Christmas morning, he informed me that I would receive no gifts from him since I had ruined our first holiday together. He held true to his word.

The second year, Sam miraculously agreed to visit my family. In fact, he suggested it himself. What I didn't realize was that he would use this opportunity to blame me for everything: traffic jams, cold weather, gifts he didn't like, even the fact that my mother didn't serve the same food his mother did for holiday dinners. These so-called offenses became his ammunition anytime I suggested we visit my family again.

Our last Christmas together was probably the most memorable because I was more determined than ever that nothing he did was going to ruin it for me. I was challenged at every turn. Miraculously, he had announced at Thanksgiving that we'd be spending Christmas with my family. My mother was thrilled, I was shocked, and one week before we were supposed to leave he came home and announced that he'd changed his mind. I knew I would have to come up with some excuse to tell my family.

I remembered my resolution not to let his actions spoil this holiday and became more determined than ever to make this a happy time. Sam refused to attend my office party and refused to take me to his. Then there was the Christmas shopping. He complained that I had too many people to buy for, but ridiculed the gifts I had chosen while trying to keep costs down. At one point he had already bought six gifts for his sister but claimed he wasn't yet finished. It was late and I was tired of being on my feet. I suggested that we call it quits for the evening. He started yelling at me in the middle of the mall, accusing me of not caring about his family. I was humiliated.

Three days of silence followed. Then I got a call at the office one afternoon, and though no one was speaking I heard bells jingling. I received four more calls that afternoon with just the sound of the bells. When I arrived at home, Sam was waiting at the front door. In one hand he held the bells and in another a Santa's hat. He had a big smile on his face, so I knew that I'd been forgiven.

Finally Christmas morning came. I was a little surprised to see that he had only one gift for me this year. When I opened it I thought it was a practical joke. It was a frying pan that he had pointed out to me during our shopping, joking that this was all I'd be getting for Christmas. But it was no joke in the store and it was no joke that Christmas morning. I kept thinking he had something hidden that he'd bring out later, especially since he had bought such extravagant gifts for his family. I was wrong.

I remember celebrating New Year's together before Sam and I were married: romantic nights on the beach, drinking champagne and watching the fireworks at midnight. Even if we'd gone to dinner or a party first, he'd always insist on leaving early so that we could bring in the year alone. He'd look in my eyes and tell me that nothing made him happier than knowing he'd have another year of loving me.

Once we were married, bringing in the new year changed dramatically. Sam didn't want to go to dinner with our friends, and he had no interest in being alone with me. He had only one preference, and that was to drink as much as possible. We'd go to a friend's house and he'd drink himself into oblivion. I was expected to be his designated driver.

One New Year's Eve while I was driving home Sam started complaining that I wasn't driving fast enough. I reminded him that I had problems seeing at night, so I was being extra careful. He covered my eyes with his hands and asked how I would like it if I couldn't see at all. Later he grabbed the steering wheel from me and started to swerve. While I was taking down the decorations the next morning and he was sleeping off his hangover, I just couldn't find an explanation for the change in him. I didn't realize that this was the real Sam, and the one on the beach years before was the Sam who desperately wanted to win me over.

Before Sam and I were married, I used to look forward to my birthdays with great anticipation. One year he planned a wonderful surprise party at one of my favorite restaurants. When I arrived I found a beautiful bouquet of flowers, a bottle of wine, and all of my closest friends waiting for me. The next year, Sam surprised me with a beautiful necklace and a candlelight dinner. After we were married, I learned to dread the innocent yet inevitable questions from friends and relatives about how my husband and I would celebrate my special day.

When my twenty-sixth birthday arrived, Sam and I had been married for only two months, and I was not in the least prepared for the drastic change in his manner of celebrating. That Sunday morning he didn't even acknowledge my birthday, and simply told me we needed to do some grocery shopping. I figured he had something up his sleeve, and he did. He wanted to buy snacks to bring to a friend's house to watch football. As we were leaving the store I finally asked him if we were going to spend any time together that day. With no explanation, he simply said no. I told him that I knew he didn't want to miss the football game, but I'd really love to have a little picnic first. He said it was too hot outside, so I suggested a movie after the game. He said there was no movie he was interested in seeing.

We arrived home and I still thought he must have something planned. Maybe this football story was just a way to throw me off. I was wrong. Since I was new in town, I had not yet established close friendships, so that night I went to a movie alone. I was confused, hurt and bewildered over the drastic change in his attitude.

Our wedding anniversaries were no better. On our third anniversary I literally begged him to go to dinner with me. He was just as averse to attending any events that involved my family. He outright refused to attend my sister's wedding or my grandmother's funeral and tried to convince me to skip them too. Special occasions had lost their previous appeal and become days I simply wanted to make it through.

In Sickness and In Health

It must be me, I thought. There's something about me that's causing him to act this way when I know first-hand he can be so supportive.

I remember the first time I realized that my feeling under the weather in any way was simply not acceptable to Sam. We had been married for about three months when I came down with a throat infection and cold. I was feeling really drained by the end of the workday that Friday, but Sam had long since established Friday evenings as laundry and grocery shopping time. I didn't want to place the burden of all the chores on his shoulders, so I started the laundry before he arrived home from work. I was sitting on the couch folding and matching his socks when he walked in. I saw a look of disgust on his face. He went into our bedroom without speaking to me. I followed and asked what was wrong. He seemed angry and demanded to know why I had an unhappy look on my face when he walked in. I was confused. I told him I probably didn't look as happy as usual because I was feeling really sick. He rolled his eyes but said nothing. For the next few hours I continued to do laundry as he watched television, silently.

Finally he suggested that we pick up some Chinese food for dinner. I thought everything was going to be just fine, but I was wrong. As soon as we got into the car he started in on me. He said he hated the way I looked when I was sick, the way my eyes drooped and I looked like I had no energy. He said he couldn't stand to look at me and that I should just go off into another room and be alone. I thought I was going to be sick to my stomach as I listened to him. I couldn't understand why my feeling sick was so repulsive to him. I tried telling him that I couldn't help how I looked, that it was normal to look this way when you're not feeling well. I told him that I had always thought we'd take care of each other when we were sick. He refused to discuss it any further.

He told me to leave him alone until I felt better and could look and act normal.

In the silent hours of that night I recalled a different side of Sam, before we were married. I remembered having a relentless cough once while we were in college. He had lovingly wrapped me up in his sweatshirt and coat. He had been so concerned that I stay warm. Then I thought back to the time I was in the hospital for a tonsillectomy. Every day he brought little gifts to me, a stuffed bear, a simple red rose. As I recalled these times, no logical explanation presented itself for the drastic change in his attitude. It must be me, I thought. There's something about me that's causing him to act this way when I know first-hand he can be so supportive.

From that day on, I tried my best to camouflage any physical discomfort, but to do so was nearly impossible. I suffered quite often from migraine headaches, which were difficult to hide because noise and light became unbearable at times. Sam could often tell if I had a migraine just from looking at me. I used to dread coming home from work at such times. He'd take one look at me and say, "Oh God, you have a headache again." He'd just ignore me until I appeared to be back to normal.

One evening during our fourth year of marriage, I simply couldn't disguise my illness. We were coming home from the grocery store and I seriously believed I was about to get sick in the car. When I told him that I was nauseated, he started laughing and driving recklessly. He jerked the car from side to side then slammed on the brakes. He said, "Go ahead and get sick, you said you were sick." I was stunned. I begged him to stop, but he just laughed harder and continued. When we finally arrived home, Sam acted as though nothing unusual had just occurred.

Laughter was as common a reaction from Sam as was disdain when I displayed any sign of physical discomfort. Once while I was jogging, I slipped on some algae on the sidewalk. Within minutes my upper leg was covered in an itchy rash. I needed to get medication right away to treat it, so I asked him to drive me to the pharmacy. He laughed uncontrollably at the whole incident, especially when I showed him the rash. I went to the store alone. The rash took several weeks to clear completely, and during those weeks he continued to tell me how gross I looked and that he couldn't bear to look at me.

I quickly learned that my being tired brought on the same disgust from Sam. Before we were married, I used to enjoy taking naps on weekend afternoons. The first time I tried this after we were married, I thought he was joking when he roused me from my sleep and stated that there would be no napping in our house. It didn't take long to realize that he was serious. If I tried to take a nap, even after thoroughly cleaning the entire house, he'd literally drag me from the bed.

One summer afternoon I had been weeding in the yard and felt a bit dizzy by the time I came back into the house. I sat down on the couch with a big sigh. That was a mistake. He reacted immediately with accusing questions: Why was I tired? What had I done that was so strenuous? Why did I look so pale and weak? There was disgust in his voice. When I told him that it's normal to be tired sometimes, he stormed out into the garage. I went out a few minutes later, hoping to clear this up. I told him I didn't understand why it bothered him so much for me to be tired. He said I hadn't earned the right to be tired, that it made him sick to see the way it took all of my energy to do the yard work. I told him how insensitive and ridiculous he was being, how no one could be human around him. He said nothing.

I was so full of anger that I had to vent it somehow, so I drove around aimlessly, radio blaring, crying. Finally I went to a park and sat in the parking lot until it turned dark outside. I fantasized that he would be at home worried about me, or that when I came home he'd greet me with open arms and say something like, "Let's just forget about all this and be happy." These were my fantasies, but not even once did they become a reality. I stayed away for as long as I could and then realized how hungry I was, so I went home. I walked into a tense silence that I knew from experience would last for several days until he decided to take me back.

The most shocking example of Sam's insensitivity in regard to my health, not to mention emotional needs, was his reaction when I had a miscarriage. I wasn't even aware that I was pregnant, and one day at work I began to have horrible cramps. I ran to the bathroom and crouched down in one of the stalls in utter agony. Suddenly I felt a rush of blood flowing out of me. I had no idea of what was happening. One of my co-workers happened to come in and insisted on taking me to the emergency room. A few hours later I learned that I had experienced an early miscarriage. I had been unable to reach Sam by phone, so it wasn't until I arrived home that he found out what had happened. He looked at me with a blank stare and asked what I would be fixing for dinner. I felt a heaviness overwhelm me, as it dawned on me that he was not joking. There would be no words of comfort, no hugs, no talk of the life that could have been.

Although being sick or tired around Sam was unacceptable, his idea of health was no picnic either. He decided somewhere in the second year of our marriage to subscribe to a fitness magazine. He became almost obsessive about counting fat grams and buying only fat-free products. Both of us were in good physical shape to begin with, and neither of us needed to lose a pound. My resistance to his idea gave him yet another area of my life over which to exert control and judgment. If we went out to eat, he'd make sarcastic comments if I ordered anything fattening, like fries or dessert. If I went ahead and ordered what I wanted he'd make comments the entire time so that I couldn't enjoy it. Our friends kept telling him that I clearly needed to gain weight, but he'd insist that I was fat and out of shape.

At one point Sam suddenly decided that I needed to lift weights with him and become more muscular. Of course, he volunteered to be my personal trainer. At first I rather liked the idea; it would mean he was spending quality time with me. I didn't even think to be insulted by his comments that I had no upper body. We started on a serious weight program, working out four to five times a week in our garage. I did get stronger, but it wasn't worth the price. He would insist that I do forced repetitions even when I told him I was pushing myself too hard. If I couldn't do as many as he thought I should, he'd start yelling at me, saying that I was a wimp and that I'd never be in any kind of shape.

One night as we were working out he pushed me to a breaking point physically and emotionally. Tears formed in my eyes, another taboo. I told him that I needed a break. He started yelling, saying that he couldn't believe I was crying. He asked me what was wrong with me that I didn't want to get stronger for him. I actually apologized and got back on the bench for another set. But he said he was too disgusted with me to go on. He hopped on his bike and didn't return for an hour.

During that time, I said aloud, "What just happened cannot be normal. I think I'm living with a sick, sick person." I remember this clearly because it was one of the first times I began to open my eyes and realistically see my situation. But I still had a long way to go. That was my last workout with Sam. When I told him that I wouldn't be lifting weights with him anymore, he looked at me incredulously and asked, "But why?" And he truly seemed to have no idea.

Weights were not the only things I was expected to lift with ease. Sam made a habit of loading me down with packages when we went shopping. It almost seems too ridiculous to be true looking back, but anytime we shopped I was expected to carry the majority if not all of the bags, and to do it cheerfully. Once when I was having trouble juggling several packages, he turned to me and said, "I hate the way you always look like you're struggling just to hold a few bags. It makes you look like such a wimp." The truth was, I was indeed struggling - not just to hold the bags, but to disguise my every struggle. Our marital vows of loving each other in sickness and in health were never to be fulfilled.

Crossing the Line

She rationalizes away his every failure, her every disappointment, and while she hides the truth from the world she also hides it from herself.
(*From* "Women Who Love Too Much")

I remember the first time I had a strange feeling that something was wrong. It was our third date, and we had just arrived back at my dormitory after a romantic dinner. We kissed goodnight and parted ways. I was about to walk inside when I felt Sam grab my arm. He told me not to go in yet, but for no apparent reason. After a few minutes of talking, I explained that I really needed to get some sleep, but he physically restrained me from leaving, claiming that he couldn't bear to part yet. I ended up staying outside with him until four o'clock in the morning simply because he wouldn't allow me to leave. I felt strange about his restraint of me, but wrote it off in the morning by reasoning that he must really love me if he couldn't stand to be apart.

The next clue was not nearly as subtle because my physical safety was at risk. It was Saturday night and we had planned to go to a nightclub in a nearby city with a group of our college friends. Sam had been drinking so I suggested that someone else drive. He became furious that I did not trust him to drive me and insisted on traveling alone. I went with our other friends and assumed things would smooth over once we all got together and began to enjoy ourselves. But once we arrived he refused to even speak to me. I made the best of the situation and started playing a game of pool with a friend from our school.

During the game, Sam approached me and asked me to leave with him. I was relieved that he wanted to make up, so I told him we could leave as soon as the game ended. But he insisted that we leave immediately. I told my friend goodbye and walked out with him, confident that we'd talk it out and everything would be fine. He was silent as we climbed into the car. He was staring straight ahead as he turned on the ignition and stated, "All I have to say is that you should never doubt me again." Then he started driving unbelievably recklessly. We were screeching around blind curves, driving in the wrong lane. He was out of control and I was terrified. I begged him to stop and he slammed on the brakes. As we came to an abrupt stop he looked at me with unwavering eyes and said, "Get out now or risk your life." I got out. He took off immediately.

It was cold, dark, and at least a mile from the bar I was now wishing I had not left so eagerly. I was too stunned over what had just occurred to cry or feel any real emotion. I made it back to the bar safely but could not bring myself to go in and face my friends. I sat on a stoop outside, rocking back and forth to stay warm. The girl I had played pool with earlier spotted me as she was leaving, and I gratefully accepted a ride to the dorm. When I arrived, Sam was leaning against my door, head bowed, crying. He apologized profusely, explaining that he had only acted that way because I had made him jealous by ignoring him at the bar. Somehow when he explained it that way, teary-eyed and contrite, it suddenly seemed less threatening, less objectionable, and much less real. And so began a series of justifications of abusive behavior that lasted throughout our relationship.

Once we were married, Sam's attitude about the abuse of women really began to surface. Whenever there was a television show involving domestic abuse, he'd insist that we watch it then turn up the volume during the most violent scenes and begin laughing. When I became alarmed he'd tell me that she probably deserved it.

Although Sam never struck me in a fit of anger, his words and behavior taught me to believe that I had something to fear and that I must always walk a careful line. And though I was never actually battered by him, the abuse took many forms in our relationship and slowly became a way of life that I learned to accept.

On any given evening once we were both in bed, Sam would tell me that he wanted the bed all to himself and that I should sleep on the couch. When words proved unsuccessful, he would literally shove me onto the floor with his hands and feet. Usually I would just fall onto the carpet, but a few times I hit my head on the edge of the wooden nightstand. Either way, he would laugh hysterically and continue to do this until I'd agree to sleep elsewhere. Then he began placing metal clothes hangers inside and underneath my pillowcase. I became so accustomed to it that it became a habit to check my pillow before ever laying down. Soon he began to place the hangers underneath the sheets for the entire length of the bed on my side. This went on periodically throughout the duration of our marriage, so clearing away all of the metal hangers before climbing into bed became the norm for me.

Many times while Sam and I were riding in the car together, he would start to pinch my arms and legs for no reason and refuse to stop. If I told him how much it hurt, he'd call me a wimp and continue. Even when I showed him the bruises later, he'd refuse to acknowledge any wrongdoing. If we disagreed about anything, even something as trivial as which movie to rent, he'd start to pinch me until I gave in and did what he wanted.

One of the aspects of Sam's abuse that bewildered me most was his need to frighten then console me. While we were still living in an apartment, we used to take long walks in the evenings along a main highway where we lived. We'd talk about how great it would be once we had a home of our own. It was a close time because we were alone, it was dark and sometimes chilly, and he'd drape his arm around my shoulder as we walked. On several occasions, Sam would suddenly remove his arm from my shoulder and start whispering to me that he would like to push me out into the traffic so that he could watch the cars run over me. He'd say that he wanted to see my brains smashed and scattered all over the road. Then he'd grab me and pretend he was going to push me out into the oncoming traffic. It was never a truly close call, but he'd make sure it was close enough to really frighten me. Then he would pull me close and hug me, and the walk would continue as though nothing had occurred. A few times I tried to run back to the apartment, but he would chase me down and force me to continue the walk.

As time went on, Sam's efforts to scare me became more and more real. During the final year of our marriage, he began saying that he'd like to suffocate me. We could be sitting around just watching television and he'd grab me by the hair and force my face down into a pillow. He would hold me there until I was in a total panic. Then he'd comfort me with a warm hug and kiss. Once he held a knife to his throat and then my own, claiming it was just a joke.

One afternoon I was taking a dip in his parents' pool. Staring at me intently, he came into the pool. Without a word, he forced my head under the water. As I began to struggle and panic, he did not let me up. By the time he did let go, I was already swallowing water. He laughed. I cried. And ten minutes later we both went in to have dinner with his parents as though nothing had happened.

Although the majority of abuse occurred behind the closed doors of our home, Sam sometimes crossed the line in front of other people, usually my friends. One Friday night I asked him to attend a cocktail hour with me. Everyone from my office would be there, and I was tired of spending every Friday night doing the ritual chores. He reluctantly agreed, then did something that ensured I'd never ask him again. Six of us were sitting around a table drinking and talking when he suddenly picked up my right arm and bit my shoulder. Everyone looked shocked. Though it did hurt, the embarrassment and humiliation caused me far more pain.

I continued to justify his behavior through a mind game I played with myself. When confronted, his alibi had always been that it was just a joke and that I was overreacting, so I learned to repeat this to myself whenever an incident would occur. This sickness became even sicker as I learned to cherish the affection and closeness that often followed an abusive incident. If he pretended to choke or suffocate me then held me close afterward, the pleasure of being held began to outweigh the pain of being frightened. A person cannot continue to be alarmed, even by alarming behavior, once it is repeated enough times.

There are probably many more incidents than I have related here, but I have long ago rewritten them in my mind as something other than physical abuse. I've noticed that movies and books about others' experiences often trigger memories I must've buried. Somewhere in my subconscious I knew that Sam could seriously harm me if he felt it was necessary or warranted. I remember realizing that it had become normal for me to lock doors behind me inside my own home, for my heart to race when I heard his car in the driveway, to wake up nearly every hour during the night.

The Good Times

[T]he good times support your mistaken belief that the ugly times are somehow just a bad dream – not the 'real him.'
(*From* "Men Who Hate Women and the Women Who Love Them")

If Sam had been cruel and abusive all of the time, I think I would've realized much sooner that I was being abused. One of the things that kept me hoping and ever confused was his ability to be loving, thoughtful and romantic and then to change at a moment's notice. Even during the good times, there was an element of danger lurking, the fear that this good mood would abruptly end and he would snatch his love away again. I think this element often made the good times seem even better than they actually were, simply because of the sharp contrast between these times and the bad times.

Sam could definitely be charming, and despite the miserable life we lived, our marriage held some loving elements. On many mornings, even before opening his eyes, he'd reach out to me and give me a long, warm hug. In fact, throughout our marriage he'd tell me he loved me several times a day. Sam also enjoyed surprising me with unexpected little gifts. Sometimes I'd find a box of candy under my pillow, a stuffed bear sitting in the front seat of my car, a new plant to decorate my office. One Valentines Day he told me he'd forgotten to buy a gift for me then left a beautiful pair of earrings under my pillow.

Every year Sam and I would attend the county fair, and his only goal was to win prizes for me. He wouldn't leave until he had some big stuffed animal to give me. We'd walk around the fairground with our arms around each other, laughing and smiling, and anyone could've mistaken us for a pair of newlyweds. Sam and I also enjoyed watching television in bed together. We'd cuddle up and watch old reruns, then drift off to sleep.

At times like these, Sam seemed like a different person entirely: affectionate, happy, loving. At times like these, all seemed right with my world. This was the feeling that I so desperately tried to recapture every time he became angry, cold and hostile. I could never piece it all together clearly. Here was an intelligent, responsible man who had so many redeeming qualities and professed such high morals. His co-workers held him in highest regard. Here was a man who had many friends, attended church every Sunday, and asked me to pray with him dozens of times. Above all else, here was a man who adored me before marriage. This man could be a perfect mate as well as a perfect monster.

It just didn't add up. I spent countless hours analyzing the situation and trying to understand what caused him to turn on me when I knew he could be so loving. I twisted myself into a pretzel attempting to behave in such a way that only the loving man would emerge and the monster would disappear forever. And in the process, I lost myself and nearly lost my will to live.

PART FOUR
WAKING UP

Beyond Depression
The spirit may die slowly, unnoticed by anyone, even the victim, if it happens very gradually and she adapts slowly.
(From "Verbal Abuse Survivors Speak Out")

I had been married to Sam for over four years. I was deteriorating on the outside and dying on the inside. I never slept for more than an hour at a time each night. I was a bundle of nerves. I had lost weight and my eyes and face had taken on a hollow look. My bones ached constantly, my scalp was itchy and dry, and I had no idea how to relax. I cried without knowing exactly why, shook a lot, and jumped at the smallest noise. Yet I continued to be productive at work, kept an immaculate house, and my friends still considered me one of the most cheerful people they knew. It wasn't that I was consciously hiding my abusive relationship from family or friends out of pride or shame; I simply didn't know that what I was experiencing was not normal. I knew it was painful and highly frustrating, but I had no frame of reference for what a healthy relationship, much less a marriage, should look like. A healthy self-esteem was foreign to me at this point in my life. I didn't realize how sick my life had become or the toll it was taking on me.

The feeling I remember most vividly was the familiar pain when I would realize that, once again, I had fallen out of Sam's good graces for some reason. The reasons no longer seemed to matter nor were they disclosed to me much of the time. The silence in our house was becoming more and more frequent, and I had begun to lose hope that I could ever make things better.

One evening Sam became angry because I hadn't taken the recycling out immediately after he asked me. He began to yell, accusing me of being unappreciative of all he did for me. I told him I'd fulfill his request in a few minutes, that I just needed a few minutes to relax. That was all it took to set him off. Once again, the wall of silence went up, but this time it stayed up for an entire month. I tried everything in my power to resolve things. I apologized though I wasn't sure what for, I begged him to talk things out with me, and I even wrote him a letter telling him how much I appreciated him. A week later I found the letter still unopened on his desk, and I tore it to shreds.

Filled with frustration, I began to jog around our neighborhood every night just to burn off energy. I'd listen to music and cry as I ran. I'd pray that this would be the night he'd take me back. He had ignored me for days, even a week before, but this was the longest stretch I had endured and I was rapidly losing hope and energy.

After a month had passed, I decided to ask Sam if he still wanted to be married to me. He didn't answer. I thought maybe he was gathering his thoughts. I stood before him for what seemed like an eternity waiting for an answer that never came. He simply stood up and left the room. I found myself sitting in the bathtub that night thinking of ways to end the pain that I didn't think I could bear and didn't realize I could do anything to change. My world had become so narrowed that I saw no way out. I wanted to end my life. I asked God to take me to heaven so that I wouldn't have to hurt my family by doing it myself.

The next day I called in sick to work. I called the pastor at our church and he gave me the number of a counselor named David. David asked me if it was an emergency or if I could wait a few weeks to see him. I told him that I wanted to die. He told me to come in at two o'clock. This was my first step toward waking up from the nightmare my life had become.

Opening My Eyes

What makes a woman vulnerable to mistreatment at home, no matter how well she functions outside, is the belief that her need for her partner's love is the most important thing in her life.
(*From* "Men Who Hate Women and the Women Who Love Them")

Ironically enough, my motivation when I went to see the counselor was not to deal with the abusive situation I was in. At that point, I didn't even remotely recognize the situation as being abusive. All I knew was that I was desperate, miserable, and emotionally and physically spent, so much so that life did not seem worth living anymore. My motivation for going was simply this: I wanted someone to tell me how to fix my situation so that Sam would love me again. I wanted a magic formula. But a strange thing happened. When I told David my story, he suggested that Sam played a large part in my unhappiness. He told me the one thing that I didn't want to hear. He said that for the situation to improve, Sam and I would have to work at it together. My heart sank. I knew Sam would never agree to anything like that. I could not count the number of times I had begged him to go to counseling with me. He swore he'd never do it.

I tried to convince David that I could make things better if only he'd tell me exactly what to do. He wouldn't of course, because he knew that nothing I did or said would change Sam's behavior. Any authentic change would require Sam's desire for it. I realized that I was only there because I'd run out of options. I had already tried everything. I'd tried giving him space, being direct, being subtle, asking, telling, whispering, yelling. But all of this had earned me nothing but pain and rejection. It was like I'd been beating my head against a brick wall for years, only it didn't feel that way because each time I had renewed hope that this approach would work. David took that hope away from me, and initially I hated him for it.

I wanted to find a new counselor who could give me a different answer, but I didn't. David began to ask me questions that no one had ever asked before, questions I certainly had never asked myself. His questions and my answers began to intrigue me, so much so that I wanted to stick around and find out what it all meant. I was seeing David three times a week and Sam had no idea. David asked me hundreds of questions about my relationship with Sam and his treatment of me. I distinctly remember the first time he suggested that Sam was abusive. I immediately denied it. Abuse was a strong, scary word that described something that happened to other people. I dismissed the notion entirely, but David wouldn't. He handed me an abuse checklist as I left that day, and I read it in my car. More than half of the descriptions fit my relationship with Sam.

Little by little David's observations began to penetrate, and my resistance to them started to decrease. Though the things I was beginning to realize about Sam were shocking and painful, they were also unbelievably liberating. It had begun to dawn on me for the first time that I was not to blame for all of this misery, and that his treatment of me was not acceptable or normal. It was as though someone had removed a blindfold I'd been wearing for years, one that I had grown so accustomed to that I no longer realized I was wearing it. My world had become so narrowed during the years with Sam that the concept of options was totally foreign to me. With these new revelations, I started to feel alive, as though I had just awakened from a long sleep. The idea of looking around my world and getting my bearings suddenly seemed very exciting!

Once my eyes had begun to open there was no closing them again, and all sorts of changes in me started occurring quite rapidly. I began talking to friends about my situation and soliciting their observations. It was amazing how everyone decided to come clean once I opened the door. Nearly all of our mutual friends shared with me the concern they had felt for years over Sam's treatment of me.

Everything began to fall into place. I started reading books about abuse and its cyclical nature as it is handed down from generation to generation until someone recognizes and ends it. I recognized myself in the stories of other abused women. I felt as if they had been observers in my home because their stories were so similar to my own.

This led me to one of the most crucial steps in my awakening: I became an observer in my own home. I took a step back and emotionally distanced myself enough to begin observing Sam from a much more objective position than ever before possible. I was horrified by what I saw. I saw a man who had no remorse for inflicting pain on the person he professed to love. I saw his selfishness, his cruelty, his mind games, his lies, his need to control, and eventually the frightened little child that lived within him. And thus began the journey out of the darkness in which I had been trapped for so long. The worst was over, but I still had many dark days ahead of me.

Dark Days
*Recognition is the hardest step; after that,
nearly anything is possible.*
(*From* "Verbal Abuse Survivors Speak Out")

The longer I observed Sam's behavior, the clearer it became that we would need professional help if our marriage was to survive. When I approached him, his reaction was the same as always. He refused to talk or even listen to my concerns. He simply walked away from me and the wall of silence was up once again. But this time, instead of crying and begging him to work things out with me, I started packing. I went through all of my personal belongings and packed up the things I knew I'd want to have with me if I needed to leave suddenly. Then I performed a detailed inventory of everything in the house that belonged solely to me and kept the list in my purse. The ironic thing is that Sam didn't even notice that I was preparing my escape right under his nose.

I walked into the kitchen one evening and told Sam that we either had to go to counseling together or I wanted a separation. I finally had his attention. I told him how unhappy I'd been, how I had become physically ill from the stress, that I couldn't live this way any longer. I told him that professional help was our only chance for saving our marriage.

This time he responded. He told me that I should be grateful for the life he had given me and that I should leave if I'm unhappy because he would never go to counseling with me and he would never change. I realized then just how much control he believed he had in this relationship. He didn't think I'd have the strength to leave and he intended to punish me for even threatening to do so.

From this conversation on, I began writing down everything Sam said. I knew life was about to get crazier and I didn't want to forget anything later. I also knew that Sam was the king of manipulation, and when he decided to turn his charm on again I would need something concrete to hold onto. I was becoming more and more aware of the mind games he'd been playing and I wanted my mind to be as clear as possible. But it wasn't easy. Sam's moods and attitudes changed at a moment's notice in the days that followed. Sometimes I was dealing with an angry, threatening man, sometimes a cold, silent one, and sometimes a frightened and confused child.

I stayed for exactly one week after the night I made my announcement. By the second day Sam had fallen into a typical silence. That night as we lay in bed he turned to me and started to cry. All he said was, "Please don't leave me." My resolve weakened somewhat. It seemed he wanted to work things out after all. I felt a twinge of hope but it was intermingled with confusion. Once again I found myself wondering which was the real Sam. The next morning when I brought up counseling again he looked at me as if I were crazy. I had to keep reminding myself that I wasn't. He kept switching back and forth between the angry man and the pitiful child.

The night before I left, I gave Sam one last chance to agree to counseling. Not only did he refuse, but he told me we should go ahead and get divorced immediately. He insisted that we go through every room in the house, every drawer, every cabinet so that he could show me what he had decided I could keep. If it weren't so sick and painful, it might have been humorous to see what he had planned to "give" me. It was pitiful. With pen and paper in hand, he listed the items that I'd be allowed to keep: two plates, two bowls, two glasses, two old pots we never used, and a lamp. He told me he'd be keeping all of the furniture, and the four televisions and two stereo systems we'd purchased together. I was almost amused, except that I knew he was serious.

Later that night, I turned on the television, and the movie *Sleeping with the Enemy* was on. Sam walked up behind me and asked in a sheepish voice, "Is that how you see me - like that abusive guy?" I turned and looked at him but said nothing. He came and sat beside me, and what happened next I will never forget. He started to cry, but he had a faraway look in his eyes as though he were somewhere else. He seemed almost oblivious to my presence as he began to talk. It was as though he had reverted to his childhood. Through his tears he said that his mother had mistreated him and his sister, and that he had tried so hard to protect Rachel. It wasn't even about us anymore. He wasn't asking me to forgive him or to stay. He was tortured by his past. I believed it was some kind of breakthrough and felt a glimmer of hope. I'd never seen him this way before, and I just knew this was the first step in confronting our problems. But when I brought it up the next morning, he honestly seemed to have no idea what I was talking about. He either would not or could not face his past.

I went to stay with friends, and less than twenty-four hours after I left, Sam called and agreed to attend counseling with me. In fact, he had already set up an appointment. At the counseling sessions, Sam's behavior proved to be as unpredictable as ever. He was uncooperative and sarcastic, yet never missed a session. During one session the counselor suggested that I move back in with him. Sam waited for me in the parking lot.

He told me that if I even tried to move back he'd make my life miserable. I simply walked away. After another session he told me I'd never find anyone with his moral character. I laughed. His words were not getting to me anymore. I imagined them bouncing off of me and fluttering to the ground, weightless and harmless. He had lost the grip over my emotions and nothing he said could really hurt me anymore.

The counseling sessions were a matter of going through the motions for me. It was therapeutic, but I already knew that I was never going back. I could only manage to end this relationship one step at a time, and I wasn't yet ready to file for divorce. I didn't have the emotional energy or the strength, not just yet.

After a few months, our counselor realized that we were getting nowhere and told us we needed to make a decision once and for all. Sam shocked both of us by stating that he wanted to work things out, but claimed he couldn't believe I was serious about counseling unless I moved back in with him. The counselor agreed with his suggestion. They both stared at me and then at each other when I refused. I was not about to take a step backward. The counseling had basically become a resting ground until I was ready to take the final step to freedom.

I began attending counseling alone with a new therapist. After a few months, I decided to officially file for divorce. It was time. Sam's attitude suddenly changed, and thus began the relentless attempts to win me back. He called constantly and begged me to reconsider. He admitted that he'd been inconsiderate, inconsistent, dishonest, even abusive. He took all of the blame upon himself and promised he'd make it all up to me if only I'd give him a chance. But his words were just empty and sad to me. I wished they could be true but I knew they weren't. He was desperate and probably believed he could change, but I no longer believed that he would.

Sam would find any reason to get me to come to the house, then beg me to sleep with him. Sometimes when I stopped by to pick up my mail I'd find him watching television while holding onto one of my stuffed animals, like a child. He mailed cards to my office declaring his undying love. On Valentines Day he walked into my office with long-stemmed red roses and tried to kiss me. It felt so foreign that I couldn't believe I had actually been married to him.

One evening I called and told Sam I'd be coming over to pick up the remainder of my belongings. He said he'd arrange to be out so that it wouldn't be awkward. I wasn't prepared for what I found. There were more than fifty notes placed throughout the house, each saying the same thing - "I love you." I felt sick. I started to cry and couldn't stop. Everywhere I turned I found more notes. I went into the guest bedroom and found all of my stuffed animals lined up with little yellow post-it notes saying "We miss you, please come home."

As I carried out my possessions I gathered up all of the notes. In the process I dropped a glass and cut my hand trying to pick up the pieces. The blood got on everything I touched but I didn't care enough to stop. There were just too many emotions running through me. The last thing I grabbed was my wedding dress, which I tossed into a garbage dumpster later that night.

The most difficult night of all was the eve of our divorce proceedings. By this time I had no energy to be angry with him, resentful of him, or anything else. A strange calmness had settled in somehow during the last few weeks before the divorce became final. We weren't arguing, he wasn't begging me to reconsider, and all of the agreements were finally signed. He asked me to come over so that we could officially say goodbye. We talked about our futures. We talked about parting on friendly terms and cooperating with each other on any remaining financial matters. Finally I got up to leave and we both broke down. He clung to me at the door and begged me not to leave. He said if I changed my mind in the courtroom the next day he'd take me back. He told me I'd have to be the one to let go and walk out of his life because he couldn't let go of me. He said I was beautiful and that I shouldn't change for anyone. I'll never forget his last words to me before I left: "If we never get back together here on earth, I'll wait for you in heaven."

I literally had to unwrap his arms from around me. He said he had one last request. He simply wanted me to wave to him as I drove away. I stumbled to my car and backed out of the driveway. As I started to drive away I slowed down, and there he was, hands pressed against the window looking like a child whose mother was abandoning him. We waved and I paused for what seemed an eternity, then I slowly drove away.

The next morning I literally woke up sobbing. I cried for the scared little boy inside of Sam and the scared little girl inside of me, for the children we would never have, for the pain I had endured for the sake of a love that had betrayed me. I was surprised that the divorce proceeding was so quick. The judge simply asked me if I was sure the marriage was irreconcilable and if I wanted my maiden name back. My lawyer put his arm around me and escorted me out. It was hard to believe that almost a decade spent together could be washed away in less than five minutes.

I wish I could say that I felt better immediately. The truth is that I fell into a deep and sometimes frightening depression. I felt a strange mixture of sadness, relief and guilt. Even though I knew that Sam was not going to change and that my staying would have destroyed me, all I could focus on was the fact that I had abandoned him. The fact that he had abused me for years seemed to take a back seat. I was haunted by visions of him being mistreated as a child. I was tortured by the memory of his face in the window as I drove away. I was getting physically sick again. An entry from my journal reveals the depth of my depression:

I can't live like this anymore. The pain is so great, yet no one understands. In fact, no one would even suspect how very deeply troubled I am. I am nauseated again. I just can't go on like this.

Final Interactions

You may find there is very little to talk about once all the cajoling, arguing, threatening, fighting, and making up stops.
(*From* "Women Who Love Too Much")

Although our divorce had been finalized, Sam and I still had some financial matters to deal with together. He always managed to convince me that we should conduct our business in person, and it took awhile for me to realize that it was an excuse to see me and exert some type of control over the situation. It was almost like he needed a fix to prove to himself that he could still call the shots. And he was manipulative enough to succeed for a few months.

My last trip to our house to endorse our tax refund check confirmed to me the lack of intimacy and the emptiness that had existed between us long before I had left him. I wrote the following entry in my journal when I returned from that final visit:

> *We didn't even look one another in the eyes. The house is still immaculate. I looked around and tried to remember feeling like this was my home, but I couldn't. I don't think I ever did. It was kind of awkward between us, but not in the way you would expect from two people who had spent so many years together. It was just empty and businesslike, not unlike our marriage so much of the time. He looks thinner and older. When I looked at his face as I was leaving, I remembered all the pain I have felt looking at that face over the years, searching it for some sign of emotion, some softness, some sign of love or understanding. But it was never there. And neither was remorse.*

Sam continued to call with excuses for why we needed to see each other, but when I refused he became more desperate than ever to have some place in my life. He'd call and tell me he had tickets to a baseball game or a concert, or invite me to a gourmet dinner at his house. I never accepted. When I finally ended my interactions with Sam once and for all, I was able to focus on myself and let the healing begin.

Learning to Live

Suddenly you find yourself not needing to justify, explain, or apologize to anyone.
(*From* "Men Who Hate Women and the Women Who Love Them")

As the depression started to lift, I simply felt numb. My counselor told me it was a normal defense mechanism when your emotions have gone to extremes too often and for too long. I wrote this in my journal:

> *When I was with Sam, I used to pray that I could control my feelings and my pain. Now I can't even find them when I want to. I don't experience the highs and lows like before, and sometimes I'm actually sad about it. I used to get so excited about little things. Now even when I'm upset about something, I don't really feel it. Even if I cry, I always know I can stop now. I am like a wounded animal. Yes, I'll heal, but I'll always walk with a limp.*

The numbness was followed by a general apathy and lack of energy. I quit reading the paper, cleaning or exercising. I spent money on whatever I wanted, let the laundry pile up, and ordered lots of pizza. No pressure, no deadlines, no rules.

Slowly my body and my spirit began to recover and renew themselves, and I felt as though I was just beginning to live for the first time. I suddenly found myself and my life very intriguing. After years of swallowing my feelings and being told they were wrong if I did share them, I was suddenly able to open up to my friends, co-workers, and family. My journal reflected the excitement and liberation I was experiencing:

I'm still marveling over how I'm just now learning to appreciate the joys of little freedoms, like shopping all alone, cooking a meal, picking out decorations for my room. I'll turn 30 in a few months, and instead of feeling older I feel younger and free at last! I don't even want a boyfriend right now. I want to be on my own for awhile. There's so much to live for! I feel empowered, like God and I are this great team plotting out my bright future.

Wondering Why
Once awareness begins, determination follows.
(*From* "Verbal Abuse Survivors Speak Out")

With my growing self-awareness and renewed zest for life came a need to better understand abusive relationships and how I had fallen into one. I read everything I could get my hands on, worked diligently with my counselor, joined an abuse survivor support group, and even took a training course to assist abused women at a local shelter.

The first thing I learned was that abuse is a universal problem. It is not confined to the less educated, the poor, or the shy, meek women of this world. For many women, becoming involved in an abusive relationship is a matter of never having been taught what to expect in a healthy one. For others, a seemingly healthy relationship subtly grows abusive as the abuser becomes more and more confident that he has an emotional hold over his partner. Although signs of abuse may be present early in a relationship, a lack of awareness of what to look for as well as a resistance to seeing such signs in someone you love may also be factors.

I also learned that the cycle of abuse is often passed down from generation to generation until someone is able to recognize it, deal with it, and prevent it from continuing. There had been so many clues about Sam's past that pointed to abuse, even outright confessions from his mother. Until I ended the relationship, I had never made the connection between how Sam was treated in his childhood and how he later treated me. I had felt so sad upon hearing about his past, but had never suspected the role it would play in our relationship. I remembered the night his mother broke down and cried as she recounted to me her treatment of Sam as a child. She said that she had beaten him for hours at a time and that she had no control over her anger. She claimed that she was reacting the only way she knew how. She described how her own parents had physically abused her and that she had resolved not to repeat the pattern but had failed. This certainly explained why Sam seemed to carry around so much anger towards women. I believe that he had no outlet for this anger, as he felt it would be wrong to hate his mother. Therefore, he unconsciously took out his anger on the woman nearest him.

I recalled the stories of Sam's mother being hospitalized for nervous breakdowns twice before Sam was even ten years old. Sam and Rachel had been forbidden to visit or even speak to their mother for long periods of time. Sam had been given the responsibility of caring for Rachel. They both told me with proud looks on their faces of how he had made her breakfast before school, braided her hair, and even given her baths. It started to make sense that Sam and Rachel would have clung to one another in an unnatural way, and maybe that was why they had so strangely seemed more like lovers than siblings.

A key turning point in any abusive relationship is the point at which the victim actually becomes aware that she is being abused. In my case, I knew I was in great emotional pain, but I had no idea that I was being abused. I thought of abused women as people with hollow faces and black eyes, women who lived in fear of being killed or maimed by their partners. I didn't realize that abuse has many faces, and that mine was one of them: the seemingly happy, well-educated, successful businesswoman with many friends, a beautiful new home, and what looked like a bright future. I have since learned that the vicious cycle of abuse is enabled to continue in large part because of the gradual brainwashing that occurs in this type of relationship. If a man who has never physically abused a woman suddenly and without warning strikes her, she cannot question her perceptions about whether this behavior is abusive. But if that same man violates her boundaries little by little, day after day – yet consistently denies any wrongdoing – she may begin to believe that it is not his behavior but rather her reaction to it that is inappropriate. This is exactly what happened to me.

When my counselor shared with me the saying "today's abuser is yesterday's victim," I realized that nothing could describe Sam more accurately. It took years for me to fully realize the extent of abusiveness I had endured and the toll it had taken on my emotional health and self-esteem. Like many abused women, I went through a period of self-blame, in which I was ashamed to tell anyone that I had stayed in such a horrific situation. The natural and understandable question from people who have little knowledge of abusive relationships is, "Why didn't you leave right away? Why did you stay and allow yourself to be treated like that?" The answer is both painful and complicated, and is probably different for every woman. Many women have been raised in abusive homes and believe that such behavior is the norm. Others are financially dependent on their partners and believe they have no choice but to stay.

In my case, I think it was a combination of factors. One was youth and inexperience. When I fell in love with Sam I was not yet even an adult. I had no idea what a healthy relationship was about. Another factor was low self-esteem. I had always felt a strong need to feel cherished and accepted, yet I had never felt like one of the crowd. Whether real or imagined, I had always felt like somewhat of an outsider, even with people who loved me. At nineteen years old, a romantic relationship seemed like a guarantee of love and acceptance that I had always longed for but had never received from my family.

I realized that I needed to look back at what had happened in my life prior to my relationship with Sam in order to fully understand how I had ended up in this situation. I noticed that all of my romantic relationships had been with highly emotional, melodramatic men, and that I had quickly grown bored with more stable, healthier partners. It was as though I needed the ups and downs to stimulate any feelings at all. Life with an abusive partner is a guarantee of inconsistencies. You experience both the loving partner and the monster day in and day out until the rollercoaster becomes your road of life. You don't even expect smoothness anymore, nor do you react to the steep drops. My unconscious motto had become "minimize pain; seek peace." The notion of being treated with respect and dignity had fallen by the wayside long ago. My journal reflected an inability to connect with an emotionally healthy partner:

> *Looking back, I don't think I've ever been comfortable in a stable, healthy relationship. I've never really been treated well by someone I had strong feelings for, yet I've never been able to generate strong feelings for those who would've treated me well.*

I would have to journey into a thousand yesterdays before I could figure out how to make tomorrow different. I didn't want to be one of those women who goes from one abusive relationship to another, each time believing that this man will be different. I had suffered enough. I had cried enough. I had struggled enough. And now it was time to find out why.

PART FIVE
LOOKING BACK

My Mother
Our emotional foundations are created by the ways in which our parents treated us...
(From "Men Who Hate Women and the Women Who Love Them"*)*

I was the third of five children born over seven years to a poverty-stricken Irish-American couple living in South Carolina. With black hair, bright blue eyes, and fair skin, my mother was striking. She was tall and slender, and looked far younger than her actual age. She seemed unaware of her attractiveness.

She was a devout Catholic and a very conservative woman who valued privacy and cared a great deal about what others thought. My mother took excellent care of our physical needs and was as consistent as anyone could be: meals were served at the same time each day, we were never late to church or school or anywhere for that matter, and our clothes were always clean and ironed. Despite the fact that we were poor, she felt it was important to stay home with her children rather than work outside of our home.

The emotional side of our relationship with her was, in hindsight, very strange. She did not like to show emotions with the exception of sadness, which seemed acceptable and preferred. She never disciplined us, never yelled or showed anger. Instead, she would quietly cry and remove herself from us if we did something to upset her. We would try to draw her out, to find out what we had done or to apologize for our misbehavior, but she would withdraw further and refuse to look at us.

She did not have eye-to-eye direct conversations with us about anything. If we needed her advice or were upset about something, we'd write it in a note and leave it on the kitchen counter. After everyone was in bed, she'd read the notes and respond, leaving the responses on the top of our clothes dressers for us to find in the morning. The notes were kind, caring, and addressed whatever it was that had troubled us. The issues were not usually spoken of further, unless we left another note for her.

In many ways, we seemed to repulse our mother. She made it clear she never wanted to eat or drink after us because of our germs, and refused our attempts to kiss her on the lips. She would turn her head and avoid our kisses, but give us a perfunctory kiss on the cheek before bed each night. There seemed to be no authentic affection between us. I remember seeing other mothers stroking their daughter's hair or gently placing a hand on their leg; this natural affection just didn't exist with us.

My mother refused to become involved in any disputes among the five children, of which there were many that crossed the line from verbal to physical. She saw incidents taking place but removed herself from the situation and left us to deal with it as we saw fit. What resulted for me was more than a decade of being ridiculed mercilessly. Why I was picked to be the family scapegoat, I don't know. I wasn't the youngest or the smallest, but I did have a vulnerability about me that was easily detected and preyed upon by my siblings. I had a skin condition that caused me to have sores and scabs all over my body during the summer months. They constantly told me I was gross and didn't want to sit next to me for fear of getting my "disease."

My brother and sister once held me down and stuffed leaves, sticks and dirt into my mouth until I started choking. My mother witnessed this but did not stop them. I never felt emotionally safe or protected in any way. I knew I was on my own.

It seemed I could never please my mother and yet I never tired of trying until well into adulthood. I felt that if I could somehow please her by being good enough, then she would find it in her heart to love me. I didn't know that a child should not have to earn the love of her parents or that no matter how "good" I became, it would never have secured the love she was unable to give. My mother had issues of her own. Her father had abandoned the family when she was a teenager and did not contact her for over twenty years. Her mother was someone who seemed impossible to please and was very critical of my mother. She spent a great deal of energy trying to defend her decisions to her own mother.

Although I can see the pattern between mother and daughter that was passed down to me, the unfulfilled longing for her love and affection was not a wound I could heal simply by understanding why it may have been this way. Trying to obtain an unobtainable love is a difficult habit to break because so much of it operates on an unconscious level. It didn't become easier simply because I was legally an adult. In fact, some of the most hurtful memories involve her disapproval of things that happened after my childhood was over but the desire to please her was not.

She tried to convince me not to go to college because she was afraid I'd change my beliefs and wouldn't be the same person she had raised. She was reluctant to help me complete the paperwork I needed to apply for financial aid, which I desperately needed since we could not afford the cost of college tuition. Her efforts to deter me might have succeeded had I not received several academic scholarships that enabled me the opportunity to attend college virtually cost-free.

I thrived at college. I made friends easily for the first time in my life. I learned to like myself and to feel I had something to contribute. One of the best things I did was to join a club where we traveled to different churches to sing. Music had always been important to me, and I was so excited when I was asked to perform a solo only a month after joining the group. Everything went perfectly during the performance, and I sent home the church program to show my mother. She responded with a long note detailing the hurt she felt because I would visit a church that was not the same denomination as ours and said that I had humiliated the family.

I had always wanted to take ballet as a child, but we could never afford it. When I started my first job after college, I found an adult ballet class and couldn't wait to sign up. When I told my mother, she got the familiar cloudy look on her face and said, "You're not going to wear those horrible tights, are you?" Once again, I felt the enthusiasm dissolve into nothingness inside of me and I never did pursue ballet. I always seemed to be displeasing, disappointing and humiliating her. I apologized constantly, but was often unsure of what I had done. I continued to seek her approval well into my adult years, and still fight an inner struggle every time I spend time with her. It has been instilled in me to feel that I am responsible for her happiness and to avoid displeasing her by having opinions that differ from hers.

I have since learned that my almost desperate desire to please her began quite early in my life. She moved into a retirement home a few years ago and gave each of her children a box full of the letters we had written to her over the years. My letters reflect almost an obsession with the need to "be good" and for her to notice this, with the hope that it would earn me the love I so desperately sought from her. At six years old, I wrote:

> *I'm not sure how to begin, but I've been trying to be good all the time. I've been praying hard to be better every day. I appreciate all you've done for me and for Daddy and the others too.*

At eleven years old, the pattern had not changed:

> *Ever since I've been eleven, and even before I was, I've wanted to try to be a lot better, but I wasn't today. So starting tomorrow, I want to try to be really good at school, home, or anywhere else.*

By my early teenage years, the growing desperation for an affirmation of love was obvious:

> *Are you sure you still love me? It seems nobody understands. I've been trying to be good since Friday. I'll try to be a lot better tomorrow. If you notice, please tell me! Please don't be disappointed or mad because of this letter. I'm always on edge, and it seems like I'm just never happy anymore. Sometimes I'm not so sure I really want to live anymore. Please don't be mad and always love me.*

I suppose my mother tried to assure me of her love at times like these. All I can remember is that she responded in some way and that I would feel a little better, but I never had that warm feeling of knowing that I was loved and that I'd never need to doubt it. It also seemed that only when I was truly desperate was I able to receive any heartfelt kindness or affection.

The reality is that my mother was dealing with a host of problems, not just letters from a child who wanted to be noticed for being good. She was facing life with an emotionally ill husband without a job and five children to raise. I do not blame her, but I do recognize that her inability to meet my needs for love and emotional support affected me in a profound way. I did not feel loved or valued as a child, which created a deep hole that I later carried with me into adulthood and into my romantic relationships.

My Father

Our fathers… are our first references for how men behave and how they treat women.
(*From* "Men Who Hate Women and the Women Who Love Them")

Although my mother did not provide me with emotional security, she maintained the only real consistency in our lives. My father was a different story altogether. Long before I was born, he had been diagnosed as schizophrenic, obsessive-compulsive, and manic depressive. He lived with us sporadically, in between time spent at a psychiatric hospital and renting a room in his father's boarding home. He never held a job for long, but was a talented musician and artist. My mother told me that he could play any instrument by ear, and that she used to love to watch him play the drums at an upscale nightclub where he worked when they were dating.

My father had a love-hate relationship with himself, and subsequently with me. For reasons still unknown to me, I seemed to be his favorite. This was a double-edged sword. It translated into a great deal of time spent alone with him. Because of his emotional instability, his moods and personality differed drastically from day to day. On the days that he seemed to love me, he loved me tremendously. He taught me to play the guitar, and we composed songs together for hours. He used to tell me that I was the most generous and giving person he'd ever met, and that I would give the shirt off of my back to help others. He said I was smart and talented, and that he loved me. On other days, he would tell me that he hated me. He'd say that I was ugly, that I looked like a boy, and that I was always in his way. It's funny how I remember both the positive and negative messages, but the negative ones feel the most real and the positives sound hollow even in the telling. I would look in his eyes and see an anger and disgust that I knew somehow I had brought on but had no idea how to dispel.

My father always asked me to lay down with him; he seemed to be tired and eager to take a nap so much of the time. He would hold me in his arms and I could smell a mixture of deodorant and tobacco. Sometimes I felt safe and cherished in his arms, and other times I felt like a prisoner. I could hear my sisters and brother outside playing and laughing, and I felt so distant from their happiness. He didn't want me to leave and told me he'd feel abandoned if I went to join the others.

He'd often cry and tell me that he was a terrible father, that everyone in the family hated him except for me, that maybe he'd be better off dead. I'd look in his eyes and see a mirror image; we were two frightened children. I tried to become the parent as best I could. I attempted to convince him that we all loved him, that life was worth living, and that I'd always be there for him. After recounting this in counseling sessions years later, I was told that he involved me in what is called emotional incest by placing me in the reversed role of being a caretaker for him.

It was impossible to predict my father's moods and behaviors, and the entire family lived on edge. One of the ways that his emotional illness manifested itself was through tortured images he carried in his mind of harming us. He felt compelled to confess these feelings in hope that they would dissipate, so he often shared thoughts and feelings that were terrifying to us. The most common were suicidal feelings. Others included his fear that he'd stab one of us to death, that he was going to kill one of my sisters with a hammer, or that he would hurt my mother. He insisted that my mother get rid of all the knives in the house so that he wouldn't be tempted to hurt us.

When he would express such fears, my mother would busily begin calling aunts and uncles and asking if we could come and stay with them temporarily. Then she would gather all of us together and tell us that we might be living with various cousins for awhile. I remember the feeling in the pit of my stomach, wondering which family I'd live with and hoping that one of my siblings would be with me. Even as difficult and unstable as things were at home, it was familiar and I didn't want to leave it.

Usually we only spent a few days away from each other, then my father would be re-admitted into the psychiatric hospital and things would be relatively calm for a few weeks or months. My mother once brought us with her to visit him in the hospital. At the time, mental illness was so poorly understood that people with widely varying degrees of illness were all placed together in one large room. We were looking for his bed, and we had to pass by many others on our way to him. Many patients were restrained and tried to grab onto us as we walked past. They seemed so much worse than our father, and I kept thinking that he didn't fit in here. I wanted to rescue him and get him safely home. He would write letters to me while he was in the hospital. I could tell how miserable he was and I thought it was my job to fix things. He would ask if I still loved him, and I'd feel guilty that he didn't know that. Somehow I felt I had abandoned him.

I recall riding home on the school bus one day and spotting my father riding his bicycle at a frantic pace down our street. Our bus driver happened to be his sister, and she noticed him too and skipped our stop. The other children on the bus kept asking us why we didn't get off at our house and we didn't know what to say. We knew it was because he had left the hospital and would probably be considered dangerous by our mother and aunt. We never went home that night. We rode around in the bus until all of the others were safely home, and then our aunt took us to her house where our mother was waiting. I could tell she had been crying, and she and my aunt whispered in the kitchen before coming out to tell us that "Daddy is feeling sick again."

All I could think about was how sad he would be when he arrived at our house and found it empty. I felt sick to my stomach imagining how abandoned and confused he must have felt. I wanted to contact him to let him know we still loved him. It was so confusing because I never knew if we were supposed to fear him or trust him. My mother used to tell us, "He'll never hurt you, but he's afraid he might, so it's better if we go away for a little while." Looking back, I feel equally sorry for her as I realize the strain she was under in trying to disguise her own fears.

It was not until I was in my twenties that I started to realize that my relationship with my father was very unhealthy and had placed me into a reversal of roles in which I had to act as the parent to this unhappy, insecure man. I was unaware that this relationship had colored my view of men and would lead me into a marriage with another emotionally ill man who would continue the cycle. After my divorce from Sam, my counselor asked me to write a letter to my father saying anything I'd like to get off of my chest. I had no idea what would come to mind but just began to write...

Dear Daddy,

I think I know why you were so mixed up. Your mom was emotionally ill and your dad was always drunk. You must've had such a hard childhood. I wish you hadn't. You deserved to be happy. We all did.

I was really unhappy too. Our life was so crazy. I'll tell you how I wish it could have been...I wish you had lived with us all the time and had a good job like other fathers. I wish we had lived in a nice house and that I had to share my room with only one sister instead of all three. I wish I could have fit in at school and could have brought home friends, maybe even had a slumber party for my birthday.

I wish I could have talked to you and asked for advice with my problems or even just help with my homework. I wish you could have attended school events and been proud of me.

> *I wish you had stopped my sisters from making fun of me all the time. No one was ever there to protect me or explain anything or help me with problems. I had to handle everything in my life and try to make you feel better at the same time.*
>
> *Most of all, I wish I could have just come to you at any time, run into your arms or climbed into your lap to tell you I loved you. But I never knew what to expect. Sometimes you said I was sweet and pretty, but later you'd say I was ugly or that I was always in your way.*
>
> *I felt so despised by everyone in the family. The only thing I could do to be worthy of love was to help you with your problems. Now I can't even love a healthy man because I only know how to love a sick man. I've been abused and taken advantage of because you never taught me I deserved better. I know it wasn't your fault, but I really wish it had been different. I deserved to have unconditional love from my parents. Now I'll just have to learn how to give this love to myself.*

It's easy to see now that I began taking responsibility for the happiness of others long before I ever met Sam. I was already accustomed to being both cherished and despised for reasons I would never understand, so Sam's treatment of me felt painful yet familiar. It did not feel foreign to me because it was exactly what I had known from the first man in my life.

Life at Home
We learned too young and too well how to take care of everyone but ourselves. Our own needs for love, attention, nurturing and security went unmet...
(*From* "Women Who Love Too Much")

The atmosphere in our home was always one of uncertainty. We never knew when my father would be living with us and what his mood would be when he was home. He could be warm and loving at times, and we seemed to feel all was right with our world. We would gather around him as he told us stories of his childhood, played songs for us on the guitar, or taught us magic tricks. But there was an ever-present awareness that things would never stay peaceful for long.

His obsessive-compulsive disorder manifested itself in a constant need to wash his hands until they bled and to repeatedly check for unlocked doors or other things he considered to be dangerous. He became very anxious and irritable during these times, and we instinctively knew that we should stay out of his way. He also became paranoid and was convinced that everyone, including us, hated him. No amount of reassurance seemed to help, and he'd quit job after job because he was convinced that his co-workers disliked him.

Since he never kept a job for long, we moved often and with very little notice. When I was five, we moved to a low-income housing complex where we stayed for about two years. We were not allowed to play outside because it was not safe, so we only ventured out for school and church on Sunday. I witnessed a good deal of violence from my perch at an upstairs window. I remember seeing a woman chasing a man with a knife. I remember a woman beating her child with a large stick and another woman pulling her daughter's hair in an attempt to drag her into their apartment.

central grassy area between our building and the next, a group of teenage boys would gather and smoke for hours in the evening. I felt a strange comfort watching them and a disappointment on the rainy nights when they weren't there.

On summer evenings when the apartment became stifling, my mother would allow us to sit quietly on the back stoop for a few moments, as long as we promised not to speak to anyone or draw any attention to ourselves. Summers were the most difficult because we had long days to fill and nowhere to go but from one hot room to the next. If my father were there, he'd just nap in front of the fan.

The apartment was infested with roaches and mosquitoes. I remember sitting at the breakfast table and feeling a roach crawling up my leg, and playing with my favorite doll and seeing one make its way out of her tiny pink mouth. We had a hard time getting to sleep at night. If we slept with no covering, we'd be bitten by the mosquitoes, but the heat was so oppressive that it was torturous to have even a light sheet on top of us. My mother was afraid to leave the windows open for fear of an intruder, so we'd lie awake and sweat, then take turns passing around a wet washcloth for our foreheads. It felt so good when the oscillating fan made its way to the bed I shared with my older sister, and the humming sound eventually lulled us to sleep. But the walls between apartments were paper thin, and my sleep was often fraught with the sounds of couples arguing and babies crying. The winters were easier because we could pile blankets on top of ourselves and I could cuddle in with my sister to keep warm. We had a tiny space heater downstairs that we would gather around to get dressed in the morning and after bath time, which I recall as a great comfort.

After a few years, we moved into a one-bedroom apartment in a slightly nicer area. Because the apartment was directly over a dentist's office, we were not allowed to run or make loud noises until evening. We had a small porch overlooking a main street, and we loved to watch the happenings on the street below. To access the apartment, we entered through a dark hallway with peeling brown paint and the constant smell of urine. Once I was coming upstairs alone when I saw some kind of figure crouched in the corner of the hall. Thinking it might have been a dog, I approached but quickly recoiled as I saw an elderly man squatting down and defecating on the floor. He looked at me with sad blue eyes and I sprinted up the stairs to tell my mother what I had seen.

One afternoon when I was nine, my father gathered us together and told us that the building was being renovated and we had received notice to vacate within thirty days. We were very happy there because we were allowed to walk up and down our street and had made friends with all of our elderly neighbors as well as a few cats. I remember my parents sitting at the table trying to figure out where we would live next. My father's youngest brother had a house in the suburbs, and was able to convince one of his neighbors to rent out a small house that had once been a real estate office. The landlord was reluctant to take on a family of seven with a father who had no steady income, but miraculously agreed to give it a try.

When my father told us we'd be renting a house in the suburbs, we were ecstatic about having a real house. We moved into the two-bedroom house and marveled at what a huge yard we now had. Although several rooms in the house did not have insulation, it was neat and clean and felt like the first real home we'd ever had. We stayed in this house for the remainder of my childhood, which provided a sense of security in an otherwise unstable situation.

The move was a step up for us but brought with it a new set of problems. Having no car, we had to rely on public transportation to get to school and church since we no longer lived within walking distance. We were attending school with children from middle-class families for the first time. The local Catholic school had accepted our family as their designated charity case for the year. Although the concept was surely developed out of kindness, it did not manifest itself that way in reality. Our family's name was given to parents with a request for clothing and assistance. I remember being handed bags full of clothing from my classmates. One of my younger sisters was humiliated when her teacher wrote "poor/no car" next to her name on the chalkboard to commend our family for attending Mass every Sunday despite a lack of transportation.

This is when I first became aware that we were poor and that our family life was vastly different from that of my classmates. During the first week of school I was asked by several students what my father did for a living, and I felt the first sting of shame when I could not answer them. I started to view myself as inferior to others, whether they perceived me that way or not. I had difficulty making friends because I felt I had nothing to offer and was embarrassed that my family needed contributions from my peers.

It didn't take long for the families at our new school to realize that my father was different, not just because he didn't have a job, but by the way he looked and acted. He had a very difficult time looking people in the eyes and an awkward gait that seemed to carry a deep shamefulness. It was almost as though he didn't think he was worthy of talking to others. Although he was quite handsome with his dark hair and brown eyes, he always wore wrinkled clothing that looked too large for him. I remember walking to church as a family and noticing the contrast between our neatly ironed clothing and his disheveled attire.

My father's behavior in public was just as unpredictable as in our home. He was once arrested for trespassing after a police officer found him lying in a church pew crying one summer afternoon. Sometimes he wandered the streets with no shoes and walked out into traffic as though oblivious. When he was living at his father's boarding home, he was once found hiding in a closet behind a rack of coats. His problems could not be hidden from the eyes of our peers no matter how much we wanted our family to appear normal.

My deepest desire at school was simply to fit in. I wanted to blend, to have a few friends I could feel safe with, and just get through this whole process of school. But that was not to be. I was keenly aware that we had been labeled as the poor family with the sick father, and I also stood out because I was so underdeveloped and small for my age. By the time I reached high school, I was still only the size of many elementary school children and was ridiculed on a regular basis.

I excelled academically despite my desire not to stand out, and thus had an excellent relationship with my teachers. I wrote poetry that was published by a national children's magazine when I was eight years old and won essay contests in middle school and high school. I won several academic scholarships that allowed me to attend college despite our lack of finances. I loved writing and learning, and the academic side of school became a bright spot throughout otherwise difficult years. I even enjoyed doing homework every day.

The social element of school gave me a hollow, gnawing feeling in my stomach for many years. I had no confidence and absolutely no idea how to reach out to make friends, so I decided to spend my lunch hours reading in the library. I remember the comfort of the quiet library with shelves of inviting books, where I could read to my heart's content and never have to face the rejection of my classmates. This worked for the most part, with the exception of the dreaded field trips and holiday parties.

Looking back, I realize that I probably isolated myself unnecessarily, and that I didn't have to spend years feeling as a loner. Because I never tried to join in with the others, they viewed me as even more different because I seemed unapproachable. At the time I felt I had no choice. It never occurred to me to share my struggles with either of my parents. The concept that I was unlovable and therefore did not deserve to be befriended by my classmates was clearly established in my mind. Asking for suggestions on how to make friends was not my focus; creating ways to survive school as an unworthy person was.

Perhaps if I'd felt some self-worth at home I might have mustered up the confidence to make friends at school, but I felt not only unworthy but actually despised within my family. This message was conveyed to me directly through my father's cruel words and indirectly through my mother's silence upon hearing them. Although I had a good relationship with my siblings whenever we spent time one-on-one, they treated me differently when we were all together and joined in my father's negative comments toward me as though it were a source of entertainment.

It quickly became a family habit to mock anything about me. I think it made my siblings feel safe because as long as I was the established target of ridicule, no negative attention would be directed at them. Having a parent participate made it even more painful for me because there was no one to tell me that their criticisms were untrue. I remember looking at my mother's face, hoping to see some sign of disapproval when they would insult me or make fun of me, but it was always a blank slate. I used to be afraid to enter our shared bedroom if two of my sisters were already inside. I felt like a helpless animal that was always preparing for the next attack. There was just no safe haven for me anywhere.

On Good Friday of the year that I was twelve years old, I was playing in the yard with my brother and sisters when my aunt and grandfather drove up unexpectedly. They looked so somber as they walked to the front door. My mother called us in a few minutes later and asked us to sit at the kitchen table. My aunt told us that my father had passed away. I didn't know what the term meant. My brother said "It means he's dead." No one said how he died. He was only thirty-nine years old. My mother stood silently at the kitchen counter as we tried to comprehend the news. That night we went about our usual nighttime routine.

The next morning, my mother showed us an article in the local newspaper saying that my father had committed suicide by overdosing on his medication. She said that she had spoken with the coroner and that only the correct dosage of medication had been found in his system. She assured us that he had actually died of a heart attack. I saw my name in the article, listed as a survivor alongside my siblings' names. It looked so strange in print.

The funeral home was crowded with people who hugged us and told us to take care of our mother. I looked at my father in the casket and thought he looked very thin and wax-like. I tried to remember what our last interactions had been like. He had been at our house just two days earlier. A few weeks before his death, he and my mother had agreed upon a visitation schedule in which he'd come to see us on Mondays and Wednesdays. That Wednesday, he called a family meeting and asked my siblings and me if we'd agree to have him visit on Fridays too. We joked around and pretended we were going to say no, feeling rather cocky that we had actually been given the power to make a decision ourselves. This went on for some time and eventually we agreed that he should visit three times a week. He seemed hurt that we had taken so long to decide and had treated his request as a joke. I felt guilty and wished we could erase what had just happened.

I had walked with him to the bus stop that night as usual, and we stood together silently, waiting to see the familiar red bus making its way toward us. We didn't kiss goodbye that day as we sometimes did. I remember him climbing the two steps to load the bus and turning around absentmindedly to acknowledge me as he heard me say goodbye. I had no idea that I would never see him alive again.

My mother remained calm throughout the funeral, but she broke down at the burial and almost collapsed. My uncles held her up and she called out my father's name as the dirt was being shoveled onto the coffin. I had never seen her so upset before. Although she cried quite frequently, it was always in a stifled and conservative way. She never seemed out of control until that day. My siblings and I all looked at each other with uncertainty in our eyes.

My father had so few possessions that everything he owned at the time of his death fit into one cardboard box. My aunts and uncles came to our house to discuss who should keep what. I received two sketches he had done, one of a candle and one of a human hand. My mother kept one of his brown flannel shirts and my aunt took the oversized sweater he wore all winter since he didn't have a coat. My brother kept his drumsticks. One of my sisters kept an empty tobacco can that he used to carry around when he smoked a pipe. We took turns sniffing it that day because it smelled just like him.

Life became significantly calmer after my father died. My classmates never mentioned anything about him to me when I returned to school after the burial, and I realize now it was because of the article about his suicide. They probably didn't know what to say. We rarely spoke of him at home, and my mother never discussed with us how we felt.

While he was alive, she had always asked us to pray that God would heal him of his illness. I remember riding on the school bus not long after his death and coming to the realization that God had answered our prayers by taking him. I just knew he was in heaven and could be happy at last.

I felt that the burden of trying to make my father happy had been lifted. I did not feel sad or miss him, and even in the absence of those feelings I knew that it was a strange reaction. Yet our family simply went on with life almost as though something traumatic and life-altering had not just occurred.

PART SIX
A NEW DAY

Getting Help
*To seek help when you need it is a sign of
courage, strength, and intelligence.*
(From "Men Who Hate Women and the Women Who Love Them"*)*

Even when we realize that our past holds the answers to why we may have ended up in an abusive relationship, it is difficult to piece it all together without help and guidance. Sometimes we find all of the answers in our past, sometimes we don't. Sometimes we stir up old memories we wish we'd left alone. But more often than not, I believe that looking back with professional help is worth the effort. It helped me to not only figure out how I had been emotionally programmed to be receptive to abusive men, but also stopped me from blaming myself for not knowing better.

Such awareness can take years to unfold. I'd be lying if I said it was an easy process, but it was definitely a liberating one. As painful as it was to go back and relive the past, it allowed me to view myself as the helpless child I was yesterday so that I could be the healthy woman I wanted to be today.

Other family members may not want to go back with you, especially if it involves talking about issues that were never dealt with or simply buried. Family members may become angry with you or deny that events ever occurred, but you must remember that this is causing them to squirm, to be emotionally uncomfortable. And maybe you're ready to deal with your shared past but they are not yet. Maybe they never will be.

Don't be discouraged if you feel overwhelmed by negative feelings when you begin to look back. Your counselor can help you deal with these and understand that it's actually a healthy sign because it means you're breaking through the numbness of buried pain and beginning to feel again! Uncovering hurtful memories is both frightening and exciting, leaving you with a sense of sadness and relief. But as you begin to understand yourself and to see the patterns your life has followed, you can reach a level of awareness you may never have thought possible.

Once you have released the guilt and responsibility from yourself, authentic growth can occur. For the first time, you can say to yourself, "There is a reason, and it's not my fault." For the first time you can say, "Now that I know, let's go about fixing it so that I never suffer this way again."

Perhaps the most significant thing I learned through counseling was that our fathers represent the first man in our lives, the one from which indelible beliefs of what a man is and should be are imprinted upon our minds and hearts. If this first man is abusive, we may easily become programmed to relate to and feel comfortable with men who strike this familiar chord with us, even when the familiarity is intermingled with a great deal of pain.

The feeling that stands out most in my memory of my childhood is that there was just no safe place for me emotionally. Nevertheless, my relationship with my father was the closest thing I had to feeling safe and loved. He needed me, I needed him, and I subconsciously learned how I would expect to be treated by a man. My marriage had held the same dimensions: a needy man who both loved and hated me. It was painful but familiar. And I had continued to seek love with Sam the same way I had sought it with my father.

My father's treatment of me instilled many distorted beliefs that I carried into adulthood and into my marriage. It taught me that a man can switch from loving you to hating you without warning or explanation; that the man who holds you in his arms and makes you feel safe can also make you feel despised; that pain is an integral part of being loved. Worst of all, it taught me that a man desperately needs to know you love him… and that you must provide this assurance at any cost to yourself. Because of that mistaken belief, I had come close to losing my own will to live.

During my counseling sessions, I was given several assignments that helped me to not only understand my past, but to refocus my attention upon myself. This was new to me because I had spent my childhood focused on my father and my marriage focused on my husband. Now it was my turn, and the unfamiliarity soon turned to an amazing sense of freedom and a previously unknown joy.

My first assignment was to write "About Me" on a blank sheet of paper and then to write anything that came to mind: my talents, my likes and dislikes, anything at all. I ended up filling up eight pages before I finally stopped in exhaustion. Next I was to write a list of all of the accomplishments in my life, no matter how trivial it might seem to someone else. Topping my list was "I ended an abusive relationship." Finally, I was asked to make a list of all of the attributes I'd like to find in a romantic partner, along with a list of what I would no longer tolerate. I was almost at a loss for the first list; I had never asked myself what I wanted before!

Learning to focus on myself for the first time was liberating and healing. The next step for me was realizing that Sam was responsible for his own behavior, no matter how difficult his past had been. I wrote the following in my journal when reflecting upon my marriage:

> *I spent a long time this morning remembering how Sam treated me for all of those years. I don't feel sorry for him anymore. I am sorry for his childhood, but I had a hard childhood too and I am choosing to be healthy. He could*

choose that too. But it will have to be with someone else, not me. He had so many chances, so many choices, yet he never treated me or even himself with the respect we both deserved as people. It's time for me to focus on myself and to trust that Sam will seek his own healing when he is ready. Or maybe he won't, but I am no longer involved in any way in his choices. What a relief. What liberation.

One of the final steps in my recovery was allowing myself to grieve the losses in my life: the childhood I never had, the love my parents couldn't give me, the love I thought I'd found with Sam, the love I had never known how to give myself. For the first few months I spent a great deal of time crying. But underneath the tears I sensed for the first time a certain distinct strength buried below the sadness – one that had taken root as I began my healing process, one that had never existed before. And at that moment, I knew that I was not just going to survive, but that I would begin to truly live for the first time.

Learning to Love
*What should feel bad has come to feel good, and what should
feel good has come to feel foreign, suspect, and uncomfortable.*
(*From* "Women Who Love Too Much")

The thought of being in another relationship scared me for quite some time. I dated occasionally but managed to keep everything casual. I was very focused on myself and my healing, and for the first time in my life was carrying no guilt over being responsible for someone else's happiness or unhappiness. I had always thought that marriage or a committed relationship would offer the security that I had longed for as a child. I knew that I was starting to heal when I realized that the secure feeling I had sought for so many years could be found within myself. It was so hard to believe that only a year earlier I had questioned whether life was even worth living!

After turning down several dates with Fred, a very attractive banker who seemed quite interested in me, I finally decided to give him a chance and invited him to join me for a drink with my friends one night after work. Fred was polite, gentlemanly, fun and easy to talk to. My friends at the bar seemed instantly at ease with him, and kept giving me looks of approval. I felt that I should have had some interest or feelings for him, but I could not conjure up any to save my life. I wanted to like him, to feel something… anything, but there was nothing stirring inside of me, so I never went out with him again. The same story repeated itself a few more times with a few more Freds.

Then came Tony. I met him at work and instantly felt something… attraction, excitement, curiosity, a connection. I wasn't looking for a relationship, so I knew I wasn't approaching this from a needy standpoint and I was proud of myself for that. But I was relieved to know that I could still feel something! Just like with Sam, Tony and I became almost instantly serious despite any of my intentions to take things slowly. But he seemed so different from Sam in all the ways that I needed. He was so loving and nurturing, taking care of me when I was sick, bringing me food and flowers and love letters. The feelings of being in love that I had not experienced for so many years now came flooding back. I was so infatuated with every little aspect of how he looked, moved, and carried himself. The chemistry between us was incredible, and we could barely keep our hands off of each other. He was so many things that Sam was not, so many things that I had needed Sam to be. He seemed to adore me.

Somewhere in the second month of our relationship, I started to see things in Tony that bothered me. It was not his treatment of me, but of other people. He was always criticizing our co-workers – saying they were incompetent, that he was the only one who knew what he was doing, even calling a close friend of mine fat and ugly. One night when we were walking on the beach I asked about his family, and he said that he doesn't get along with his sister because "she's a bitch." I was so shocked.

I wasn't sure if I was being overly sensitive or paranoid because of my past. But I kept thinking that one day this ugly side that I was starting to see bits and pieces of would be directed at me. It wasn't very long before my fears were realized, even though it was only in small ways at the beginning. One Saturday morning I was reading a book on intimacy that my counselor had recommended. He took one look at the cover and said, "Oh, another psychobabble book?" The night before I had shown him my master's thesis and he had laughed at it. He said he couldn't believe that they'd give someone a master's degree for writing about animals. Then he saw the hurt look on my face and apologized profusely. Both times I felt a twinge of familiar discomfort. I knew he wasn't trying to hurt me, but I knew I was feeling hurt nonetheless. I decided to pay attention to the twinges.

I soon started to feel taken for granted. Tony would call and expect me to bring him dinner almost every night. He rarely said thanks when I did little favors for him like returning a movie or helping him fold laundry. He seemed to expect to be taken care of and resentful when I resisted. I finally told him how I felt, which was a big step for me. I was using the skills I had learned in counseling: expressing my true feelings in a respectful way and expecting to resolve the problem together.

It seemed to work at first. Tony apologized and seemed to change his attitude, but only for a few weeks. As we were lying in his bed one lazy afternoon, it seemed like a good time to talk to him again about how I was feeling taken for granted. Our arms were intertwined. When I told him what I wanted to talk about, he immediately pulled his arm away from mine and sort of threw my arm back onto my chest. I felt something stop inside of me as though to tell me to take note. It was like he was on the edge of being abusive but not quite there. I got up and walked out of the apartment and he followed. He said he was feeling hurt because I hadn't called him the day before, that he felt like I was always criticizing him and that I make him feel insecure. I told him I wanted to be alone so that I could think. A few hours later, Tony showed up at my house with flowers and a card, apologizing and telling me that he couldn't have made it through the night until he knew everything was right between us.

I knew Tony wasn't treating me with the respect I deserved, and I felt that I was seeing red flags everywhere. Here we were only a few months into the relationship and he was blaming me for his behavior, a familiar song. But it seemed so hard to believe that I could have chosen another abusive man after all of the counseling I had done. How could Tony be so different from Sam and yet exhibiting so many of the same behaviors?

Things continued to deteriorate. Tony became so possessive of me that he was listening to my phone messages, looking at my calendar, even trying to read my journal. He became very critical of me, accusing me of being a flirt, calling me selfish and bitchy. Just like Sam, he could also be just as loving, affectionate and complimentary as he'd been in the beginning.

I had to ask myself what I was getting out of the relationship that was keeping me hooked. The only answer that made any sense was that it felt so good to be loved during the good times. I realized that I was putting aside things that didn't sit right with me in my relationship with Tony, important things like respect and consideration for my feelings. I was willing to do so because I wanted the intimacy and love that he had to offer, and it came in a package that I could connect with.

Why could I only feel that connection with men who treated me poorly, who were inconsistent in their feelings, even highly critical of me? This is the question that brought it all to light. It was familiarity that I craved. I had bonded with Tony instantly, just like Sam, because they struck that familiar chord of my relationship with my father. Familiarity feels like a connection, and a connection feels like love… at least for awhile.

Never had the expression "the truth shall set you free" held so much meaning as it did upon this realization. I looked at Tony and I saw a future too close to my past. I saw a road I had already traveled down, crawled down, cried and stumbled down. It was a road I would not go down again. Whether I would ever be able to be attracted to a healthy man I didn't know, but I did know that I'd be fine whether that ever happened or not. I had healed.

***

The Beginning.

If you can relate to what you have read, be it from personal experience or perhaps someone you know, visit our website for additional resources.

Visit:

http://www.aurorapublishinginc.com/authorbio_ar.html

Postscript
In My Eyes

Postscript

In My Eyes

It has now been 13 years since I left Sam, and today I am a different person altogether. I am physically and emotionally healthy, and I have a stronger self-esteem than ever before. I can hardly believe the turns my life has taken since leaving Sam, allowing myself to heal, and ultimately learning to trust again.

I am now married to a wonderful man I had known as an acquaintance for years before we actually started dating. Perhaps I felt a little safer with him because he wasn't a stranger to me, so I accepted the invitation when he first asked me to join him for lunch.

I could tell right away that Michael treated women with respect and dignity, and it didn't seem he was just trying to make a good impression. He was funny, intelligent, sincere, and anything but pushy. In fact, we continued to go to dinner, movies, and the beach for well over a month before things became romantic. I grew to know him slowly and gently, and the more I knew him the more respect I was gaining for him as a person and a potential partner. We shared so many of the same interests and values, and just seemed to "click." There were no awkward silences in our conversation, yet I didn't feel he was trying to win me over or impress me in any way. He was just being himself.

I started to feel very comfortable and emotionally safe with Michael. I never felt I had to be on guard or looking for red flags. It was easy to just be myself; there was no need for game-playing or pretensions. I shared with him the entire story of Sam, my childhood, everything. He was so supportive and nonjudgmental.

My descriptions of Sam's behavior shocked him. I knew then that Michael was an entirely different man from Sam or any of the others I had dated.

Our intimacy was not instant. Instead, it blossomed over time but grew with leaps and bounds as we became closer over the first year that we dated. I think we both knew that we wanted to marry each other, but we took our time. We still went out with our friends on a regular basis, never gave up our hobbies or favorite pastimes, and simply enjoyed each other's company as we grew closer.

This type of relationship was so new and refreshing to me, but it brought with it some difficulties. Because I had always experienced such an adrenaline rush with the dangerous, rocky relationships, I thought maybe something was missing in my relationship with Michael. I sought the help of my counselor once again, and she explained to me that I had become addicted to the highs and lows of abusive relationships and would probably be uncomfortable initially with one that didn't hold such elements as nagging doubts, volatile arguments, jealousy and control. She was so right. I wasn't accustomed to being happy and content in a relationship!

About 18 months later, Michael and I married. We honeymooned on a beautiful tropical island in the Caribbean and soon bought a house together. We wanted to have children right away. I had never been happier. Our relationship held all of the elements I could have hoped for in a marriage – romance and friendship intertwined, a solid sense of trust and emotional safety, shared values and beliefs, and a feeling that all was right with my world.

After a few years we decided to look into adoption since I had not conceived, and I had always wanted to adopt a baby. After a difficult year of case after case falling through, we were blessed with a beautiful, healthy baby boy. Being able to see Michael as a father just added to my respect and love for him. He participated in everything from baths to changing dirty diapers to middle of the night feedings. He was a true partner in every sense.

A few years later, we started talking about adopting a sibling for our son. I shared with Michael a dream that I had started having from the time I was 17 years old, of a tiny, dark-haired girl who was handed to me in a small box. I knew in the dream that this was not my biological child, but I knew as surely that this tiny girl was indeed my daughter. I never saw the face of the person presenting her to me, but always heard the same words – "she needs you." I had continued to have this dream several times every year for my entire adult life.

At about the same time, Michael's brother was undergoing major surgery in California, so he flew out to be with him. He called me from a mall a few days later and told me about all of the beautiful little Asian girls he had seen. I had expressed an interest in adopting from China a few months before, and he took this as a sign that we should proceed.

I started all of the paperwork and could hardly contain my enthusiasm. We were approved for adoption in October. That night we went out for Chinese food to celebrate, even though we knew we were still in for a long wait before we'd be matched with our new daughter and travel to China. Later, we found out that the very night we had celebrated was our daughter's birthday!

Seven months passed and we received the magic call telling us that we'd been matched with a beautiful little girl. A few months later we traveled to China. I'll never forget the moment she was handed to me by the orphanage director – it was instant love. A few days later I had the opportunity to visit the site at which our daughter had been abandoned. It was a remote area where she could have so easily not been found. As I stood marveling at how this had all come about, I noticed that the orphanage director held a paper with a series of Chinese characters written on it. I asked what it said and as the words left my mouth, I already knew what the answer would be. She told me that our daughter was found abandoned in a small box – just like my dream. I started crying uncontrollably. They were tears of joy and amazement.

Our daughter is now a year old and our son is four. Michael and I have been married for almost eight years, and our relationship is as solid as ever. The past often seems more like a bad dream than reality.

I wish I could say that the pain of the years with Sam has disappeared altogether, but abusive relationships tend to leave lifelong scars in one way or another. Sometimes I still have flashbacks and nightmares. Sometimes painful memories pop up when I least expect it. Perhaps there is a part of me that will always feel the pain of the past, but Sam and his distorted reality are no longer a significant part of my life. Love doesn't hurt anymore. I have truly learned to live "in my eyes."

Appendix A

Abuse Checklist

What is Abuse?

<u>Physical Abuse</u>

Does your partner:
- Hit, slap, shove, choke or kick you or your children?
- Threaten or hurt you with a weapon?
- Throw objects at or restrain you?
- Abandon you or lock you out?
- Hurt you when you're sick or pregnant?
- Force you to have sex against your will?

<u>Emotional Abuse</u>

Does your partner do things that shame, ridicule or insult you, like saying:
- You're stupid, fat, ugly, etc?
- You can't do anything right?
- You'll never get a job?
- You're an unfit parent?
- You don't deserve anything?
- Who'd want you?

<u>Other Abuse</u>

Does your partner:
- Threaten to hurt your child or pet?
- Forbid you to work?
- Control all the money and force you to account for what you spend?
- Humiliate you in front of others?
- Accuse you of having affairs?

- Keep you from family or friends?
- Confuse you with promises, lies?
- Take your keys, damage your car?
- Take or destroy personal property or sentimental items?

*If you or someone you know could answer "yes" to even some of these questions, help is available through counseling, support groups, and shelters.

(Source: Women in Distress of Broward County, Inc.)

Appendix B

Finding Help

There are organizations in every state in the United States to help abused women. You do not have to be physically battered to receive these services.

Call the Domestic Violence Hotline at **1-800-799-7233** (open 24 hours) to find a program or service agency in your area.

Calling for help could save your life.

Appendix C

What to Bring If You Leave

If you have time to <u>safely</u> gather belongings, consider taking the following:
- Your cell phone and charger
- Cash
- Phone numbers of family, friends, and shelters
- Credit and debit cards
- Keys (including all sets to your car)
- Personal papers for you and your children (life and health insurance information, birth certificates, marriage license, social security cards, your will, address book, tax return copies)
- Account numbers and balances (checking, savings, investments)
- Identifying information on your partner (social security number, date of birth, employer address and phone number, recent photos)
- Any documentation of abuse (photos, copies of police reports, etc.)
- Your journal/diary

Other steps to take:
- Find out which accounts you have access to and if they are in both your names.
- Find out if you are both listed on any mortgages.
- Notify your employer of your situation and identify a plan for what to do if your partner shows up at your place of employment.

Place safety above all other considerations.
All of the above are replaceable, but you are not.

Appendix D

Recommended Reading

Books

Dugan, M.K., and Hock, R.R. (2000). *It's my life now: Starting over after an abusive relationship or domestic violence.* New York: Routledge.

Engel, B. (1990). *The emotionally abused woman: Overcoming destructive patterns and reclaiming yourself.* New York: Ballantine Books.

Evans, P. (1996). *The verbally abusive relationship: How to recognize it and how to respond.* Avon, MA: Adams Media Corporation.

Evans, P. (1993). *Verbal abuse survivors speak out.* Holbrook, MA: Bob Adams, Inc. Publishers.

Forward, S., and Torres, J. (1986). *Men who hate women and the women who love them: When loving hurts and you don't know why.* Des Plaines, IL: Bantam Books.

Loring, M.T. (1998). *Emotional abuse: The trauma and the treatment.* San Francisco: Jossey-Bass, Inc.

NiCarthy, G. (1982). *Getting free: A handbook for women in abusive relationships.* Seattle: The Seal Press.

Norwood, R. (1985). *Women who love too much: When you keep wishing and hoping he'll change.* New York: Pocket Books.

Websites

www.domesticviolence.org

www.womanabuseprevention.com

www.sylviasplace.com

www.webheights.net/GrowingbeyondEmotionalAbuse

www.lilaclane.com/relationships/emotional-abuse/links.html

Learn more about Allison Richards by visiting:

http://www.aurorapublishinginc.com/authorbio_ar.html

She welcomes your questions and invites you to visit her blog.

Additional information on emotional abuse and helpful links are available on the website.

We welcome your thoughts and suggestions.

Thank you.